Alvin H. Hansen is Lucius N. Littauer professor (emeritus) of political economy at Harvard University. In addition to teaching, he has served as Director of Research and Secretary of the Commission of Inquiry on National Policy in International Economic Relations (1933–34); member of the Advisory Council on Social Security (1937–38); Chairman of the economic advisory council of the National Industrial Conference Board (1938–1939), and special economic advisor to the Federal Reserve Board (1940–45).

Professor Hansen is a member of the American Economic Association (vice-president 1937, president 1938); the American Statistical Association (vice-president 1937); the Royal Economic Society; the Econometric Society. He was also a member of the Social Science Research Council from 1934 to 1936 and from 1937 to 1941.

He was a member of the board of editors of the *Quarterly Journal of Economics* from 1937 to 1948; he has also been on the editorial boards of *Review of Economic Statistics* since 1938, *Inter-American Economic Affairs* since 1947, and *Kyklos* since 1947.

D1264556

By Alvin H. Hansen

The Postwar American Economy

PERFORMANCE AND PROBLEMS

ALVIN H. HANSEN

LUCIUS N. LITTAUER PROFESSOR OF
POLITICAL ECONOMY, EMERITUS, HARVARD UNIVERSITY

The Norton Library

W · W · NORTON & COMPANY · INC · *New York*

Contents

Preface

This little handbook is intended to give the general reader, as well as college students, a survey of the four recessions and recoveries which we have witnessed in the American economy in the period 1948–1963. This includes, in addition to statistical materials, an analysis of the new (and old) forces that produce economic fluctuations, together with an appraisal of the impact on the cycle of the Kennedy Administration tax proposals.

The first two recoveries were buoyant; the second two anemic. The first two cyclical upswings carried the economy close to the full-employment ceiling; the last two lacked "steam," leaving the economy, even at the "peak" levels, considerably below the country's growth potential.

One of the two full-fledged recoveries came in the Truman Administration; the other in the first Eisenhower Administration. One of the two weak recoveries came in the second Eisenhower term, and one in the Kennedy Administration. But the Kennedy recovery has turned out to be a long recovery, though well below full-employment levels.

Public policy was not the main factor. Spontaneous forces, rather than deliberate policy, account for the high-level employment and rapid growth in the first two recoveries. These automatic expansionist forces exhausted themselves and remained at a low ebb throughout the period of the last two cycles. So long as the expansionist forces dominated, unemployment averaged over the entire period of the first two cycles only 4 per cent of the labor force. Once these forces subsided, however, the unemployment rate rose to an average of 6 per cent in the two-cycle period 1957–1963.

Now we are about to witness, we hope, an exciting new venture. At the moment when this Preface is being written, we do not yet know what Congress may or may not do. A bill is being pressed by the Administration in Congress designed to forestall the recession which past business cycle experience tells us may be imminent early in 1964. The bill if passed would make a major cut in individual and corporate income taxes, amounting to about $10 billion per year—this cut to be implemented in two installments, the first to be effective in January 1964 and the second one year later.

If the bill finally passes the Congress and is signed by the President, it will be the first time, as far as I know, that the U.S. Government has carried through a program *in advance,* designed to *prevent* the next recession. We are familiar with programs designed to halt a recession that has already reached serious proportions. But never before have we undertaken an anti-recession program while recovery was still on the way.

It could be an interesting spectacle to observe how it might all come out. The tax cut might indeed do the trick so far as 1964 and 1965 go. But it is likely to take much more than this to conquer, once and for all, the age-long recurring periodic recessions.

What are the probable limits within which the tax cut may prove to be effective? This problem is analyzed in Chapter 3. And what further policies will be necessary to keep full "steam" up (over the longer-term trend) in the economic boiler? Chapter 4 discusses economic growth in theory, and Chapter 5 discusses practical policy on inflation and the balance of payments, as well as the relations of these two currently burning problems to the business cycle.

It appears evident, based, to be sure, on limited experience, that the postwar business cycle swings have become more moderate. Credit for this would probably be given by most students of the cycle to the built-in stabilizers. Rapid growth trends, especially in Western Europe, have profoundly influenced the pattern of postwar cycles. In the United States, however, there is a tend-

ency on the part of business forecasters to relate cycle movements
to the previous peak rather than to the potential growth trend.

For college students, it is hoped that this handbook may
serve as useful supplementary reading in courses on business
cycles, money and banking, macroeconomics, and economic history.

Alvin H. Hansen

November, 1963

*The Postwar
American Economy*

1 · The Four Postwar Cycles

The Cycle New and Old

Following the First World War, several leading economists voiced the belief that the business cycle had vanished for good. And after the Second World War some expressed the view that continued and sustained prosperity was here to stay. By now, however, experience has demonstrated beyond doubt that the cycle of production, income, and employment is still with us.

The cycle is indeed in some ways a new kind of phenomenon. The basic interactions are the same, yet something new has obviously been built into the economic structure. The "rocking chair" doesn't rock in quite the old familiar way.

Some things are much the same. For one thing, investment in inventory stocks continues to play a very important role. Fluctuations in investment in fixed capital (new construction and producers' equipment) have toned down. In consequence, we have had no truly *major* cycle in the postwar period. But a new actor in the cycle drama, or at least one that has by now assumed a leading role, is the federal budget.

A Changing Capitalism

If, however, one turns one's attention away from the minutiae of cyclical interactions to the great tidal waves of historical changes and their impact on the economy, and so upon the nature of business cycles, one cannot fail to note that we are indeed living in a new world. The last three decades of the nineteenth century were a period of great territorial expansion, massive immigration, transformation of a rural society into an industrial society, the growth of huge corporations and vast fortunes. It was not a stable society. Price upheavals, boom, bursts of prosperity, unemployment, bankruptcies, deflations, "now prince, now pauper"—these were the order of the day; millionaires and slums—vast wealth, squalor and poverty. Still, Americans for the most part retained a middle-class status; they operated small family farms and small family businesses. But growing industrialization pressed more and more illiterate immigrants into ever-growing cities. A labor class (foreign to American tradition) and a labor movement developed, still largely outside the pale of the law. An unbridled capitalism flourished.

A progressive income tax and a Federal Reserve System had been built into the economic structure just in time to help finance the First World War. Collective bargaining was weak; and while efforts were made to strengthen the competitive system and hold back the growing power of trusts, combinations, and monopolies, for ten years after the First World War unbridled private capitalism held sway, virtually unchallenged by either labor or the government. The untrammeled excesses that ensued ended in the great stock market crash of 1929 which ushered in the devastating depression of the nineteen-thirties.

That depression changed the face of America. Railroads, banks, state and local governments went broke. Homeowners, farmers, and small businesses became bankrupt. The federal government was compelled to bail them out. New Deal reforms were introduced—the Securities and Exchange Commission, guarantee of bank deposits, social security for the aged, unemployment insurance, minimum wage laws. A vast salvaging operation was undertaken, together with expansionist measures involving housing, rural electrification, and public works. Eventually, recovery got under way. But it was a superhuman task and many mistakes were made. There were still 9.5 million unemployed when the Second World War broke out in Europe.

War and Postwar Developments

The European war boosted United States exports, and soon the nation itself became involved. Before the Second World War was over, nearly half our productive resources had been drawn into the struggle. Unemployment vanished. The country came out of the war rich in monetary assets and monetary savings and desperately short of consumers' durables, houses, business plant and equipment. This laid the groundwork for a vast postwar prosperity which continued (with two short interruptions) until 1957. In the meantime, the Korean war added still more fuel to the burst of prosperity.

After 1957, progress continued, but at a slower pace. The whole fifteen-year period 1948–63, however, shows a degree of stability and growth rarely, if ever, matched at any time in our history. The standard of living rose steadily. Per capita consumer expenditures, after correcting for price changes, increased 30 per cent from 1948 to 1963, or 2 per cent a year. The "social dividend" (private consumption plus government civilian outlays) increased every year, including the recession years. Compared to the turbulent history of the nineteenth century and the disastrous nineteen-thirties, the period 1948–63 must be regarded as one of high stability and growth. But gradually, high-level prosperity was slipping. The unemployment rate was rising. Recoveries were becoming short-lived. The cycle was running down.

A broad general picture of economic fluctuations and trends in the last fifteen years can be obtained from Figure 1. The curve here presented—gross national product in real terms—discloses fluctuations with peaks in 1948, 1953, 1957, 1960 and troughs in 1949, 1954, 1958, and 1961. A careful inspection will reveal a sharp upward trend from 1948 to 1956, and a marked slowing down in this rate of growth from 1956 to 1963. This matter will be discussed in some detail.

Troughs, Peaks, and Time Spans in Four Cycles

The peaks and troughs of each of the four cycles are as follows:

	Pre-recession Peaks	Troughs	Recovery Peaks
First cycle	November, 1948	October, 1949	July, 1953
Second cycle	July, 1953	August, 1954	July, 1957
Third cycle	July, 1957	April, 1958	May, 1960
Fourth cycle	May, 1960	February, 1961	?

In this chapter, each cycle is labeled by its recession trough. Thus the first cycle is referred to as the 1949 cycle; the second, as the 1954 cycle; the third, as the 1958 cycle; and the fourth, as the 1961 cycle.

From the table, the time span of each cycle, from its pre-recession peak to the subsequent recovery peak can readily be calculated. The 1949 cycle, from peak to peak, ran for 4 years and 8

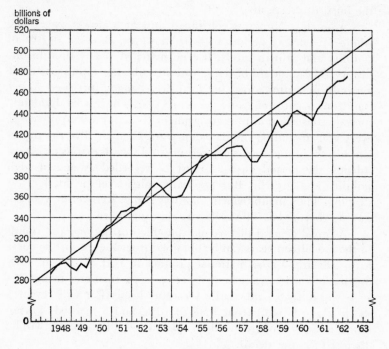

FIGURE 1. *Gross National Product (at 1954 prices)*

months; the 1954 cycle ran exactly 4 years; the 1958 cycle 2 years and 10 months (an abnormally short cycle), whereas the 1961 cycle bids fair to run a more normal length.

The time span of the recession phase was approximately similar for all the four cycles—11 months, 13 months, 9 months, and 9 months, respectively. The expansion phase, however, varied greatly. The 1949 recovery ran for 45 months; the 1954 recovery,

35 months; the 1958 recovery, only 25 months; and the 1961 recovery, it is hoped, will run a more normal period. Indeed, perhaps for the first time, a strong effort is being made, months in advance, to forestall a recession altogether. Many, perhaps most, professional economists believe that this could be achieved. But Congress is reluctant to act before the recession has actually occurred. Some Congressmen have said they would favor a tax cut *after* a recession is clearly already upon us, but not in advance of a downturn.

Each cycle is characterized by circumstances peculiar to itself. The 1949 cycle was prolonged and buoyed up by the Korean war, and its termination in 1953 was closely associated with the cessation of hostilities. The 1954 cycle, in the recovery phase, was swayed by a burst of business investment and consumer acquisitions of durables (cars, household electrical appliances, and furniture). In part these outlays represented advances in technology; in part, catching up on accumulated shortages. The 1958 cycle was peculiar in that it had two jagged peaks caused by abnormal inventory developments incident to a strike by steelworkers in 1959. The recovery phase of this cycle, moreover, was cut short by a sharp curtailment in federal budget expenditures from $80.3 billion to $76.5 billion. Finally, the incomplete character of the 1958 recovery may have contributed to the mildness of the downturn that followed, beginning in May, 1960.

Relative Severity of the Four Recessions

Among the various criteria of severity, employment and production indexes probably give the clearest answer. We have two over-all measures of production: (a) the index of industrial production and (b) the GNP in real terms (i.e., at constant prices). Both point to the 1958 recession as the most severe. The GNP in real terms declined by $22.1 billion; the index of industrial production fell by 14 per cent. The unemployment rate rose from 3.6 per cent of the labor force to 7.5 per cent (seasonally corrected).

Why was the 1958 recession so severe? The preceding investment spurt was clearly overdone. Investment in producers' plant and equipment rose by 40 per cent from a level which was already high. Consumers' durables jumped nearly 25 per cent in one year, automobiles 37 per cent. These rates were not maintainable. Offsets to the subsequent decline were nowhere in evidence. Accumulated shortages, emerging from the two wars and from delayed technological advances, had, for the most part, been filled. The time was ripe for a pretty sharp drop ($9.6 billion) in producers' investment in plant and equipment.

In the 1954 recession, the GNP in real terms fell by $13.7 billion. The index of industrial production fell 10 per cent, and unemployment rose from an average of 2.9 per cent for 1953 to a quarterly high of 6 per cent in 1954.

The 1949 recession was on balance not very different. The industrial production index fell by 9 per cent and the GNP in real terms by $7 billion. Unemployment rose from a 1948 yearly average of 3.8 to a quarterly high of 7 per cent in 1949.

Both the 1949 and the 1954 recessions were followed by long and buoyant recoveries. The 1949 recovery was, of course, fed by the Korean war; the 1954 recovery, by a burst of private investment.

In contrast, both the 1958 and the 1961 recoveries enjoyed nothing that could remotely be called a boom. The recoveries were incomplete and fell far short of reaching full employment. Whereas the first two cycles registered, at their pre-recession peaks, unemployment rates around 3.5 per cent (or less in the best quarters), the last two cycles displayed unemployment rates of around 5 to 5.5 per cent at their pre-recession peaks.

In one important respect, the last two cycles were very different. Although the 1958 decline was the most severe of all four cycles, the 1961 decline was the mildest. The index of industrial production in the 1961 cycle fell by only 6 per cent, and the GNP declined by only 2 per cent. Unemployment however increased by 2.1 percentage points. But although the decline was mild in terms of product, the 1961 cycle started the downswing from a low performance peak. The unemployment rate at the pre-recession peak was nearly 5 per cent and the GNP in real terms was running some $30 billion or more below our historically determined potential growth trend.

Both the 1958 and the 1961 recoveries turned out to be anemic —equally unable to reduce unemployment to an acceptable level. The unemployment rate for the entire peak year 1960 was 5.6 per cent, and again 5.6 per cent for 1963.

Under favorable employment opportunities, the labor force tends currently to grow at the rate of 1.3 per cent per year, and the potential increase in productivity per worker is estimated by the Council of Economic Advisers as 2.7 per cent per year.[1] This would put our potential rate of growth at 4 per cent per annum. Indeed a line on a ratio chart drawn through the GNP (in real terms) for 1948 and 1956 (both years of good employment, but not over-employment, rates) discloses a 4 per cent (compounded) growth rate. On this basis, the GNP record in the last two cycles has run some $50 billion below the full-employment level. Thus although the 1961 recession was mild, as measured from the pre-recession peak, the bottom of the recession was low, as measured from the potential growth trend.

Expansion vs. Semistagnation

The weakness of the last two recoveries becomes painfully evident when we compare the last six years (1957–63) with the preceding eight years (1948–56). Table 1 presents the data on output; Table 2 on employment, income, and profits. It is evident that the growth rates in terms of output were far stronger in the period 1948–56 than in the period 1957–63.

These tables show how dynamic the period 1948 to 1956 was, and how stagnant the period from 1957 to 1963. Cyclical com-

TABLE 1

Percentage Increases in Output

Period	GNP (in constant dollars)	Industrial Production Index	Durable Goods Output (in constant dollars)	Industrial Production Index of Durable Manufactures
1948–56	38.0	46.0	50.0	55.0
Increase per year	4.7	5.7	6.2	6.9
1956–62	18.0	6.0	9.0	13.0
Increase per year	3.0	1.0	1.5	2.2

---

[1] *President's Economic Report*, 1962, p. 113.

parisons alone fail to bring out this important point. In the period of the last two cycles, employment, income, and output had dropped substantially below the economy's potential. The gap between actual performances and the potential growth trend was widening.

TABLE 2

Increases in Employment and Income

Percentage Increases

Period	Total Employment	Personal Disposable Income (in constant dollars)	Corporate Profits before Taxes	Unemployment Rate (average per period)
1948–56	9.5	37.0	36.0	4.3
Per year	1.2	4.6	4.5	
1956–62	3.5	18.0	14.0	5.6
Per year	0.6	3.0	2.3	

Counter-cyclical Policy

The first two recessions were cushioned by substantial reductions in federal tax rates. Specifically, a tax cut, amounting to about $4.7 billion [2] was made in 1948, retroactive to January of that year. This involved large refunds in mid-1949. This tax relief no doubt helped to soften the downturn, and the economy began to turn upward in November, 1949.

Similarly, fairly large tax cuts were introduced in the 1954 recession. Effective January 1, 1954, the excess profit tax (designed to help finance the Korean war) was repealed. Personal income tax cuts were made, and excise taxes reduced in April, 1954. Altogether, the individual and corporate tax cuts amounted to about $7.4 billion.[3] This was, however, partly offset by increases amounting to $1.4 billion, in social security taxes.[4]

---

[2] A comparable figure (in terms of the magnitude of 1963 GNP) would be about $10 billion.

[3] In terms of 1963 magnitudes, this would be about $11.5 billion.

[4] *Economic Report of the President*, 1963, pp. 69–70.

In the recovery phase of each of the first two postwar cycles, substantial increases in federal spending began early in the upswing and continued on through into the period of extended expansion. Thus, in the 1949 recovery, the administrative budget expenditures rose from fiscal 1948 to fiscal 1949 by $6.5 billion and (by reason of the Korean war) averaged a per annum increase of $8.6 billion from 1949 to 1953. In the 1954 expansion, budget expenditures rose by $4.6 billion from fiscal 1955 to fiscal 1957, and cash payments to the public rose by $9.5 billion.

Early in 1957, these latter expenditure increases gave rise to heated discussion about the impending 1958 budget. Treasury Secretary Humphrey openly attacked the President's budget, and the President in turn ordered the Budget Director to resurvey the proposed expenditures. Senator Byrd urged a $5 billion cut, and leading business organizations asked for cuts ranging from $5 billion to $8 billion. Defense contracts were in fact restrained, and by September, business analysts were pointing to defense cutbacks as responsible for the unfavorable turn in the business outlook.[5]

But the policy quickly shifted from restraint to methods of coping with the recession which began in July, 1957. This new turn of affairs called for expansionist measures. More powerful still in causing a policy turnabout was the impact on defense spending occasioned by the spectacular Russian achievement in orbiting Sputnik. These events weakened the powerful political pressures demanding fiscal restraint. Budget expenditures increased by $2.4 billion from fiscal 1957 to fiscal 1958.[6]

Nevertheless, the deflationary forces which had been gathering proved to be overpowering. The heavy inventory decline (already overdue) was reinforced by a severe drop in fixed capital outlays together with a decline in consumers' durables. The 1958 downswing came on with full force. Tax receipts fell off sharply and this, together with the increased spending (the fiscal 1959 budget ran $9.0 billion above 1958), produced a deficit in fiscal 1959 of $12.4 billion—an unprecedented peacetime figure.

These budgetary developments stirred up a strong political

---

[5] Wilfred Lervis, Jr., *Federal Fiscal Policy in the Postwar Recessions,* p. 195.
[6] The increase was $4.2 billion from calendar 1957 to calendar 1958.

movement by fiscal conservatives to reverse the spending and deficit trend. A determined effort was made to balance the budget in fiscal 1960. Fiscal restraint was energetically applied, and this time the administrative budget was actually cut back from $80.3 billion in fiscal 1959 to $76.5 in fiscal 1960. This sharp reversal no doubt played a major role in cutting short the brief recovery which reached a peak in May, 1960, after only 25 months of expansion from the trough of April, 1958.

The Kennedy recovery from the February, 1961, trough did no better in its first two years than the previous recovery. Private housing starts, after 24 months of recovery, stood no higher relative to the trough low than in a corresponding period of the 1958 recovery. Employment and the index of industrial production and personal income had risen even somewhat less; and the rise in the GNP in real terms was about the same. The unemployment rate, after falling to 5.3 in July, 1962, stood at 6.1 in February, 1963, and at 5.9 per cent in May, 1963.

With this two-year record of poor recovery behind it, the Kennedy Administration early in 1963 offered a new program—a program designed not only to move the economy on toward full employment and its long-term growth potential, but also to forestall a threatening new recession. Two years before, upon first assuming office, the new Administration had pinned its hopes on a strong recovery based on an upward surge of private investment. This was to be sparked by an investment tax credit and by new Treasury guidelines permitting faster depreciation rates on fixed capital assets. A critical Congress delayed passage of the tax credit until late in 1962, so that two years had gone by before these investment incentives could begin to operate. How effective they would prove to be remained problematical. At any rate, by early 1963 it appeared evident that something more was needed. The Administration then proposed a drastic tax cut of $13.5 billion, applicable to both individuals and corporations, and spread out over two or three years. The tax-cut plan, however, included reforms looking toward a broadening of the tax base (accomplished primarily by restrictions on deduction allowances). These reforms, if enacted, would have brought in an estimated $3.5 billion of new revenue, leaving a net tax cut of about $10 billion.

The Built-in Stabilizers

Thus far, we have been discussing various discretionary, deliberate, or contrived fiscal programs, such as tax cuts and increased expenditures. But these have not always been introduced with a view to stabilizing the cycle though, on occasion (as in the case of the 1948 tax reduction), they have helped by accident to achieve that result. Quite apart from discretionary action is the automatic stabilizing effect of new institutions built into the social structure—new mechanisms tending to promote stability. The built-in stabilizers can operate with force only because of the enormously increased role of government expenditures and tax revenues. While total governmental cash payments to the public—federal, state, and local—amounted in 1929 to only $10 billion in an economy producing $100 billion of goods and services, in 1962, governmental cash payments (including the trust funds) amounted to $160 billion in an economy of $555 billion.

These increased expenditures have been more or less offset by increased tax receipts. But the ratio of expenditures to receipts varies greatly over the cycle, and the changes in this ratio can be very significant when the aggregates are as large as they have become in the postwar period. Indeed it is the change in the ratio of expenditures and receipts that constitutes in essence the so-called built-in stabilizers. In the recession phase, tax receipts fall off, while expenditures, such as unemployment compensation, relief, etc., rise. In the recovery phase, revenues rise rapidly, indeed more rapidly than GNP, owing partly to the progressivity of the individual income tax and especially to the sharp cyclical fluctuations in corporate profits. A cushion is thus placed under a recession and restraint is imposed on the upward movement. The economy is more or less stabilized.

In earlier periods of our history, the swings were more violent. Recessions were deeper, but the forces making for recovery were unrestrained. Now the "stabilizers" choke off both the recession and the boom. This may leave us on the average over the entire cycle as far from full employment as formerly. But at least greater stability has been achieved. There still remains the problem of full employment and a growth rate equal to our potential. The built-in stabilizers will not by themselves ensure full employment.

It is indeed quite possible that we could drift further and further away from our potential growth trend from cycle to cycle. The problem of adequate growth has not been solved. A solution awaits more effective *discretionary* action and long-range development planning.

Aggregate Shifts in Expenditures and Receipts

The *actual* shifts in expenditures and receipts are partly the result of the automatic built-in stabilizers and partly the outcome of deliberate policy decisions with respect to expenditures and tax rates. The accompanying table shows the actual shifts (built-in and deliberate) in expenditures and receipts (quarterly data) in the four postwar cycles: (a) from the previous peak to the trough, (b) from the trough to the succeeding peak.

Changes in Federal Expenditures and Receipts
(in billions: national income accounts)

Period	Expenditure Changes Downswing: Peak to Trough	Upswing: Trough to Peak	Changes in Receipts Downswing: Peak to Trough	Upswing: Trough to Peak
1949 cycle	$+ 3.4	$(+37.2)	$−6.5	$(+33.8)
1954 cycle	(−11.6)	+12.3	(−9.1)	+19.3
1958 cycle	+10.6	+ 0.7	−6.9	+23.3
1961 cycle	+ 9.8	+13.5	−6.2	+16.2
Average (excluding figures in parenthesis)	+ 7.9	+ 8.8	−6.5	+19.6

Excluded from the *average* figures given at the bottom of the table are the shifts in expenditures and receipts due to the Korean war and its termination. The "average" figures thus represent shifts occuring under more or less normal conditions.

Excluding the cut in expenditures in 1954 owing to the cessation of the Korean war, we note that in all the other downswings expenditures rose. In both the 1958 and 1961 cycles, the increase was about $10 billion from peak to trough. This expansionist effect was *reinforced* by a decline in receipts of around $6.5 billion in each downturn (omitting the special case of the cut in taxes in 1954). Thus the cushioning or sustaining effects of expenditure changes and shifts in receipts amounted to about $16.5 billion in the case of the last two cycles and to about $14.5 billion when the 1949 cycle downturn is included. These cushions prevented the cumulative downturn which characterized "pre-New Deal" depressions.

In the recovery phase of the cycle deliberate increases in expenditures contributed substantially to the upswings following the 1954 and the 1961 troughs. But this expansionary impact was more than offset by the automatic increases in receipts. Thus the actual fiscal program (built-in and deliberate combined) exercised a restraining influence upon the recovery movements. Cyclically, the swings in receipts play a tremendous role.

In the downswing, both tax and expenditure changes cushion the recession. But in the upswing, they offset each other: taxes restrict and expenditures expand. Taking account of both taxes and expenditures, the cushioning effect on the downswings has been more powerful than the net restraining effect on the upswings.

Social Priorities, the Level of Spending, and the Level of Tax Rates

Broadly speaking, over-all fiscal policy involves two types of decisions. One has to do with the goal of full employment; the other, with social priorities.

The second policy decision has to do with the problem of allocation of our productive resources. How much shall be employed to fill the needs of the public sector? Shall we use more of our resources for education, retraining programs, schools, hospitals, urban renewal, mass transit systems, slum clearance and public housing, etc. The amount of expenditures in any society will, of course, be guided by the prevailing social values. Decision-making with respect to social priorities constitutes the first step in a fiscal policy program. In our democratic society, the final decision is necessarily made by Congress and the President, but what they will do will be guided by the cultural and educational standards of the entire nation. Historically, we know that government expenditures have pursued a fairly steady upward trend in a growing and increasingly urbanized society.

The expenditures being determined, it then becomes the function of fiscal policy to regulate the flow of private spending so as to achieve full employment of labor and capital resources. This is the function of the tax structure. Tax rates should be adjusted, cyclically and trendwise, in such a manner that aggregate spending, public and private, will match the potential aggregate supply of goods and services which the nation is able to produce. Tax rates should be high enough to prevent inflation and low enough to permit full employment.

But is this not precisely what the monetary authorities are supposed to do: to regulate the money supply and the rate of interest so as to prevent inflation on the one hand and to promote full employment on the other? That is indeed the case. Unfortunately, we have found that monetary policy is not sufficiently powerful to do the job. Monetary policy is a necessary tool, but not a sufficient tool. Happily we have at last come to take for granted a system under which the Federal Reserve Board is given complete power over our money supply. Formerly, the delegation of such vast powers to a monetary authority was regarded as unthinkable. Similarly most people would regard it as unthinkable to entrust the regulation of the tax rate to a Fiscal Authority. The time will come, however, when we shall likewise take this for granted. Such an Authority, precisely as in the case of the Federal Reserve Board, would operate within the pattern of the democratic process.

Tax-rate adjustment has long been advocated by economists. In 1962, however, this proposal at last made its appearance on the stage of practical politics. President Kennedy in his 1962 budget message asked for legislation enabling the President, within limits imposed by Congress and subject to congressional veto, to adjust tax rates so as to promote full employment and price stability. Alternatively, this power could be delegated to a Fiscal Authority similar to the Federal Reserve Board.

Congress might legislate the administrative framework within which the Fiscal Authority would act so as to provide a semiautomatic system of tax-rate adjustment guided within limits by agreed-upon criteria of employment, industrial production, and prices. The basic rate would be fixed by Congress; the Fiscal Authority would regulate (within the established limits) the deviations from this rate. As an accepted policy instrument, such deviations should cause no surprise; indeed they should be expected as routine performance precisely as is now the case with Federal Reserve interest-rate adjustments. Perhaps these tax-rate adjustments should be restricted to the first income tax bracket where they can readily be tied in directly to our system of collection at the source.

Monetary Policy in the Postwar Cycles

Monetary policy has played a role, though a modest one, in all four postwar cycles. In the usual case, the Federal Reserve System has sought to provide monetary ease in recession periods and monetary restraint in the later stages of expansion. Reserve ratios were cut in the 1949 recession and were raised to check undue expansion in 1951. Again in 1953, at the very beginning of the downturn, reserve ratios were lowered. In the 1958 downturn, open-market purchases of United States government securities lifted the outstanding volume of Federal Reserve Bank credit, thereby enlarging the monetary base (member bank reserves) which regulates our money supply. Similarly in the 1961 downturn, monetary ease was effected by means of open-market purchases.

Monetary ease appears to have been particularly helpful in the 1954 recession and in the subsequent first phase of the recovery. Monetary restraint appears to have been applied too rigorously in the 1959–60 recovery. This, together with the fiscal restraint of the sharply reduced 1960 budget, no doubt partly explains the short-lived and incomplete expansion of this cycle. From 1958 to 1960 there was no increase at all in the money supply. Both the fiscal and the monetary restraints were in large part inspired by an exaggerated fear of inflation and by a genuine balance-of-payments crisis.

In the 1961 recovery, a strong effort was made to employ

monetary policy to help boost the recovery. Inflationary pressures were no longer imminent, and a new monetary approach was introduced to help meet the balance-of-payments problem while at the same time promoting economic expansion. An open-market and debt-management program was designed to keep the short-term rate relatively high (at least 2¾ per cent) and the long-term rate relatively low. This result was in some measure achieved by means of (1) open-market purchases by the Federal Reserve of longer-term securities in order to raise the price of such securities and thereby lower the long-term rate while, on the other side, it sold short-term securities in order to lower their price and so raise the short-term rate; and (2) Treasury issues of short-terms instead of long-terms, the effect being to lower the price (and so raise the rate) of short-terms, thereby helping to prevent the exchange into gold of dollar holdings by foreign central banks and treasuries.

The effort of the monetary authorities to influence the fluctuations and trends of the economy can be indicated in a fairly meaningful way by the following signposts of monetary ease and restraint:

1. Changes in the money supply (currency and demand deposits)

2. Changes in velocity, i.e., GNP ÷ M
3. Changes in the rate of interest
4. Open-market purchases
5. Changes in reserve requirements

For five years following the Second World War, the money supply remained nearly constant. War-financing had overdosed the economy with money, and with general price and wage controls in effect, the velocity of circulation had fallen. As GNP rose in the first postwar years, the economy was growing up to its expanded money supply. With the burst of activity associated with the Korean war and the 1951–53 expansion, the money supply again began to rise along with a moderate increase in velocity.

Up to the end of the Korean war, the economy suffered no monetary shortage. The quantity of currency and demand deposits increased by 15.8 per cent from 1949 to 1953, or 3.9 per cent per annum. In the same period, the GNP in real terms increased by 27 per cent, or 6.8 per cent per year. But the money supply, used somewhat more intensively, was on balance adequate. Interest rates (AAA bonds) rose only moderately from 2.7 per cent to 3.2 per cent.

The period of semistagnation from the mid-fifties on witnessed, however, a fairly drastic slowdown in the rate of increase of the money supply. From 1955 to 1962, the money supply grew by only 9.4 per cent, or 1.3 per cent per year. In a society with a growth potential of 3.5 to 4.0 per cent per year, the money supply could be expected to grow at more or less (though within rather wide limits) the same rate, and if one may judge by past history, even a greater rate. An increase of 1.3 per cent per year suggests an unduly tight monetary restraint. Even from 1960 to 1962, the rate of increase was only 2.3 per cent per year. The rate of interest on high-grade bonds rose from 3.1 per cent in 1955 to 4.3 per cent in 1962. The rate of discount of the New York Federal Reserve Bank rose from 1¾ per cent in August, 1955, to 3 per cent in 1962.

Defining the income velocity of money as the ratio of GNP to currency and demand deposits $\left(\dfrac{\text{GNP}}{\text{M}} = \text{V}\right)$, we find the following changes in the intensity of utilization of money over the last three decades. This table pretty much tells its own story.

Year	$\dfrac{\text{GNP}}{\text{M}} = \text{V}$
1929	3.9
1940	2.4
1948	2.3
1956	3.1
1962	3.8

A Theoretical Note: The Consumption Function and the Postwar Cycles

In a theoretical discussion of the secular and cyclical consumption functions, the author has prepared a chart that discloses the long-run secular relation of consumption to income, and also the short-run cyclical relation.[7] It is repeated here as Figure 2a.

---

[7] See Hansen, *Business Cycles and National Income*, W. W. Norton & Company, 1951, p. 165.

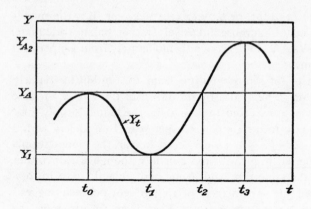

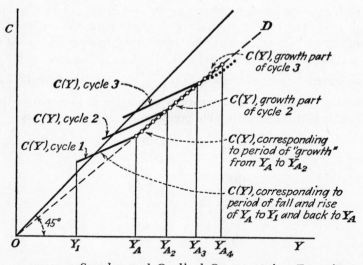

FIGURE 2a. *Secular and Cyclical Consumption Functions*

The secular curve is drawn through the peaks of three successive cycles. Cyclically, as income falls after the peak is reached, consumption falls also, but not back to its former position in relation to income. A new standard of consumption once achieved resists the downward pressure caused by the fall in income. Thus the cyclical consumption function is relatively flat. As income gradually moves back to its former level, consumption responds slowly. Thus in the recovery phase, $\frac{C}{Y}$ is relatively large compared with the smaller peak $\frac{C}{Y}$. Once the former income level is again achieved and the growing economy moves forward to new high levels of income, the secular ratio of C to Y is progressively restored. During the downswing, saving was cut into in order to maintain as nearly as possible the former consumption standard. Now when recovery has at last restored the former high income level, the habitual ratio of saving to income again becomes possible of realization. From there on out, as income reaches up to new levels, the habitual or secular ratio of C to Y is restored.

The theoretical analysis just referred to was presented without giving it any empirical backing. But now let us get a picture of the actual behavior cyclically and secularly, of the relation of C to Y in the post-Korean period. Figure 2b presents a highly interesting empirical confirmation of the earlier theoretical model. When we draw a line through the peak points we see that it is

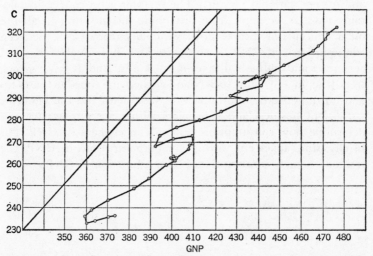

FIGURE 2b. *Secular and Cyclical Consumption Functions: The Post-Korean Period*

substantially straight, starting (if extended) at the point of origin. This line gives us the slope of the secular consumption function; given the parameters of the system as we find them in the post-Korean period. The ratio $\frac{C}{Y}$ is approximately 67/100.

A curve drawn to fit the points from the first recovery quarter to the peak represents the cyclical consumption function for each cycle. This curve is much flatter than the secular consumption function curve. But it becomes progressively steeper as it approaches the next cycle peak. The built-in stabilizers have no doubt exerted a flattening impact upon the consumption function compared with earlier periods in our history. Particularly, note that as shown in the chart, the consumption function is even flatter in the downswing phase of the cycle than in the first phase of the recovery, and much flatter than in the second recovery phase.

In this chart, GNP is used to represent income, and we have accordingly defined the consumption function as the relation of C to GNP. But it could also be defined as the relation of C to (a) disposable income, (b) personal income, (c) national income, and (d) net national product. The relation is, of course, increasingly loose as we move from disposable income through all the other concepts of income until we finally reach GNP. Between consumption and GNP lie corporate and individual saving and corporate and individual taxes of all kinds. And as GNP grows, trendwise, in a dynamic society and at the same time fluctuates up and down cyclically, the impact of these taxes and the behavior pattern of business and consumers with respect to saving will determine how consumption responds to changes in GNP. Put briefly, since taxes and saving are both functions of GNP, the residual, namely consumption, is also a function of GNP.

2 · *Spontaneous Factors and Deliberate Policy*

In Chapter 1, we employed the device of dividing the post-war years into two periods: (a) the period of rapid expansion, 1948–56, (b) the period of slack demand, 1956–63. In the first period, powerful spontaneous forces were at work *automatically* generating a high level of aggregate demand. These forces were weaker in the second period. In the first period, prosperity just happened; in the second it had to be contrived. This, for the most part, we failed to do. Unemployment averaged only 4 per cent in the first period; 6 per cent in the second. The growth rate was 4¼ per cent per year in the first period; 2¾ per cent per annum in the second.

The autonomous developments of the first period included (1) the backlog of construction; producers' durable equipment and consumers' durables left from the Second World War and not fully made up until around the middle fifties; (2) the Korean war and the cold war which followed; (3) the population increase, growth of large cities, new products and techniques representing years of technological advance which the Second World War, and to a degree also the Korean war, had pushed aside for later development.

The force of these expansionist factors in 1948–56 and their decline in 1956–63 can be measured by (a) gross private domestic investment, (b) purchases of consumers' durables, and (c) defense expenditures.

All three are "spontaneous" in the sense that they are not the product of heated partisan debate and political discussion. The first two are determined by market forces, the third essentially by external international forces which only military experts can even pretend to evaluate. The prolonged and difficult process of decision-making or deliberate policy is therefore scarcely involved to any appreciable degree in any of these three cases.

The data for these "spontaneous" factors for the years 1948, 1956, 1962, and 1963 (I) are as follows—all in billions of dollars (1962 prices):

Year	Gross Private Domestic Investment	Consumers' Durables	Defense	Total
1948	$59.5	$25.9	$16.8	$102.2
1956	74.5	40.1	46.8	161.4
1962	76.2	47.6	53.0	176.8
1963 (I)	76.8	50.0	56.6	183.4

The percentage increases per annum for each of these three "spontaneous" factors are as follows (data in 1962 prices):

Factor	Percentage Increases per Annum	
	1948–56	1956–63
Gross Private Domestic Investment	3.1	0.4
Consumers' Durables	6.8	3.4
Defense Expenditures	22.4	2.9
Total	7.3	1.9

Private investment moved forward at a fairly satisfactory rate (3.1 per cent) in the first period but dwindled in the second. Consumers' durables made a tremendous advance in the first period—100,000,000 household electrical appliances were installed. But the rate of growth dropped to one-half in the second period. Defense naturally receded after Korea and the rate of increase declined to the moderate rate of 2.2 per cent per year in the second period.

Was not general consumption (durables excluded) also a prime determinant of the relative rates of expansion in the two periods? Broadly speaking, the answer is "No." Consumption remained throughout closely tied to disposable income. There was indeed a moderate downward shift in the consumption function from 1948 to 1956. Far from making the first period expansionist, the shift put a moderate brake upon the general buoyancy. The function rapidly shifted up again, settling down at its historical normal position. These shifts—first down, then up—conformed to the expected adjustments induced by the aftermath of war. But the shifts were relatively small. Although durables (in reality goods of capital type) played an important role in the expansion of the first period and in the slowdown of the second period, the consumption of non-durables and services remained throughout closely dependent upon changes in disposable income. To this, one must make one important qualification: moderate *cyclical* fluctuations occur in consumer debt. Consumer borrowings flatten out in the recession phase and begin to rise again fairly early in the recovery phase.

So much for the "spontaneous factors" in autonomous developments. Now how about the discretionary or contrived factors, in other words, deliberate policy? These include federal civilian expenditures and transfer payments, and state and local expenditures of funds raised by themselves (excluding expenditures financed out of federal aid).

The distinction between "spontaneous factors" and deliberate policy measures is of the highest importance. In the United States, the Employment Act of 1946 places responsibility upon the federal government to promote maximum production, employment, and purchasing power. In essence, as far as full employment and optimum use of productive capacity is concerned, the federal government has been made the "lender of last resort," so to speak. If market forces provide full employment, good and well. The government then has little to do with respect to the problem of full employment, though there remain other problems, such as social insurance for old age and health, problems relating to distribution of income and to urgent public needs. But the full-employment goal as such would have been met automatically without deliberate governmental policy. If the market forces (spontaneous factors) do not provide full employment, then the government, according to the 1946 act, should step in. The problem for the government becomes very difficult, however, if the "natural" or autonomous factors making for prosperity are weak. Governmental policies in a democratic society are made by the President and the Congress. Congress represents a wide variety of opinion. Debate, conflict, and finally compromise eventually emerge. Whether or not a given period will prove to be expansionist or stagnationist will depend very much upon the potency of the spontaneous factors. Only if a government has reached a viable consensus on an appropriate fiscal and monetary policy, and perhaps also on planning programs, can one expect a high score of performance. It requires a good deal of doing in terms of deliberate policy to achieve satisfactory goals if the spontaneous forces or autonomous developments for expansion and growth are weak.

Government Civilian Expenditures

Federal civilian expenditures, as here used (total administrative budget outlays excluding defense and interest), include a wide range of public services, such as education, health, welfare, veterans, housing and community development, grants-in-aid to state and local governments, space research and technology, natural resources and agriculture, transportation and commerce, subsidies to the Post Office and other government enterprises, and general government. It is astonishing, considering the broad range of areas covered, how relatively small the aggregate figure for civilian expenditures is.

The absolute figures are as follows, in billions of dollars, 1962 prices:

Year	Federal Civilian Expenditures (defense and interest excluded)	State and Local Government Expenditures (from their own funds)	Total: Federal, State, and Local Governments
1948	$18.0	$21.5	$39.5
1956	18.0	34.6	52.6
1962	28.4	47.7	76.1

The percentage rates of increase per annum, are as follows:

Type of Expenditure	1948–56	1956–62
Federal Civilian Expenditures	0.0%	9.7%
State and Local Expenditures (own funds)	7.6	6.3
Aggregate: All Governments	4.1	7.4

Adding together the three spontaneous factors and the two discretionary or deliberate factors we get the accompanying tables, in billions of dollars, 1962 prices:

Year	Spontaneous Factors	Discretionary Factors
1948	$102.2	$39.5
1956	161.4	52.6
1962	176.8	76.1

Percentage Rates of Increase per Annum

Factors	1948–56	1956–62
Spontaneous Factors	7.3%	1.6%
Discretionary Factors	4.1	7.4
Weighted Aggregate	6.4	3.0

The spontaneous factors (strong in the first period and extremely weak in the second) were indeed partially offset by the discretionary factors. Still, as the weighted aggregate figures show, the combined effect of both sectors was more than twice as expansionist in the first period as in the second. The spontaneous factors, being three times as large in absolute terms as the discretionary factors, dominated. The weakness of the large spontaneous sector left a job too big for the discretionary factors, at least for a country not firmly committed to full utilization of deliberate policy to ensure full employment. The net effect was a sluggish economy for the second period.

The Role of Government Outlays

In absolute figures, private investment and consumers' durables each gave the economy a forward push of $15 billion in the first period, and defense stood $30 billion higher in 1956 than in 1948. In the second period, expansion slowed down to a $2 billion increase for private investment, $7.5 billion for consumers' durables, and $6 billion for defense. In both periods, defense played twice as powerful an expansionist role as private investment. In the discretionary sector, state and local governments outdid the federal government. The federal government, in its civilian outlays, provided no expansionist impact whatever in the first period and only $10 billion in the second. State and local governments pushed ahead with $13 billion in each of the two periods. These figures, it should be remembered, are all in *real terms*. The state and local figures include only expenditures financed from their own funds, the federal grants-in-aid being included in the federal civilian outlays.

The state and local governments' postwar record of expenditures is often cited on the optimistic side of the balance sheet when an attempt is made to assay future expansionist factors. Considering the constitutional restrictions and other limitations confronting local governments, the record is a pretty good one, considerably better than one might have expected. The increases in public school attendance and the increased enrollments in state-supported higher institutions of learning, the doubling of motor vehicle registration from 1948 to 1962—these are indicative of the pressures upon reluctant governments to meet urgent public needs. In 1960, two-thirds of all state and local expenditures went into education and highways. Moreover, the Great Depression and the Second World War accounted for a large backlog of deficiencies to be met in sewage disposal plants, water supply, streets, government office buildings, mental hospitals, reformatories, etc. Considering the accumulated backlog of urgent needs, a minimal part of which could no longer be deferred, the state and local increases in expenditures become easily understandable. And the pressures will continue for years to come because of the rapid growth of urban populations.

The sharp increases in taxes and borrowing, such as have in fact come since 1948, have given a severe jolt to many citizens. Sudden increases are not easily absorbed into the habitual pattern of family budgets. All through this period, average incomes were also rapidly rising. Nevertheless, a rising percentage of income was being taken by state and local taxes.

Property, sales, and income taxes collected by state and local governments rose from 5.3 per cent of personal income in 1948 to 6.6 per cent in 1956 and to 8.0 per cent in 1962. In the meantime, federal personal income taxes took 9.1 per cent of personal income in 1948, 9.7 per cent in 1956, and 10.4 per cent in 1962.

The *percentage* of income left after taxes did indeed decline, but not as much as most people might suppose. The good side of the picture—the absolute rise in income—is always less impressive than the bad side, namely, the increase in taxes. But after deducting all taxes, federal, state, and local, and after correcting for price changes and for the increase in population, we find that the *per capita* private consumption *in real terms* increased 30 per cent from 1948 to 1962, an increase of 2 per cent per year. This represents a gain in the standard of living, measured by per capita consumption in real terms, which is quite in line with our best long-term records in the past. We have achieved this average gain in the last fifteen years despite the very large diversion of our productive resources to defense and despite an average unemployment rate of 5 per cent for the entire fifteen-year period.

The foregoing discussion, however, is not quite fair. It seemed to assume that the standard of living can properly be judged entirely in terms of private consumption. But public services also contribute to the standard of living. Tax money is not just money poured down the drain. It purchased education, highways, streets, hospitals, national defense, etc., etc.

Taking an over-all view of the economy as a whole, government—federal, state, and local—absorbed in round numbers 10 per cent of GNP in 1929, 20 per cent in 1948, and around 25 per cent in 1962. But military expenditures (including expenditures directly related to war, such as outlays for veterans and interest on war debt) account for most of the increase. Military expenditures (as just defined) took 1 per cent of GNP in 1929, 10 per cent in 1948, and 12.5 per cent in 1962. Civilian expenditures took 9 per cent in 1929, 10 per cent in 1948, and 12.5 per cent in 1962—no great change, be it noted, between 1929 and 1962.

It is a striking fact that one-half of all civilian expenditures in 1962 by federal, state, and local governments went into education and highways. The remainder was expended in a long list of public services, such as those previously outlined. Clearly, no civilized community can exist without these outlays. Show me a country with a low level of public outlays and I will show you a low-standard country. We have sad examples of this in some of our low-standard states.

Per capita personal income increased sufficiently from 1948 to 1962 not only to pay increased taxes and permit a 30 per cent rise in per capita private consumption in real terms but also to permit a continuing high rate of personal saving. Consumers have saved, year in and year out, around 7 per cent of personal income after taxes. In 1962, this represented an annual saving of $26 billion. These savings went into private life insurance, private health insurance, savings deposits, building and loan associations, etc. In addition, $25 billion was paid into publicly administered social insurance trust funds. In 1962, Americans poured $50 billion dollars into what the Life Insurance Institute termed "personal protection programs"—a billion dollars each week.[1]

The Role of State and Local Governments

Many of the rich northern states, hard pressed to increase expenditures on education, hospitals, public welfare, state parks

[1] *Life Insurance Bulletin,* February, 1963.

and recreational facilities, complain that they cannot find the money to supply widely recognized public needs. A little inquiry into the facts will disclose, however, that things are not quite that desperate, at least as far as the richer states are concerned. In many of our poorer states, the problem is indeed a serious one, and federal aid is urgently needed. There remains a wide spread in per capita personal income between the rich and the poor states, but this spread is happily narrowing. In 1938–40, the average per capita income in Mississippi, Arkansas, Alabama, North and South Carolina was $249, exactly *one-third* of the average per capita income ($748) in the five rich states, New York, California, Illinois, Connecticut, and New Jersey. By 1959, the five poor states had risen to an average per capita income of $1,346, or *one-half* of the $2,664 income of the five rich states. The poor states are gaining but they have a long way to go.

In the case of some of the richer northern states, tax revenues as a percentage of aggregate personal income are relatively low compared with the national average. And so also, unfortunately but understandably, are their standards of public service.

Fifteen or so of our poorer states offer, as could be expected, low standards of public service, basically because of low fiscal capacities. Even though a heavy tax burden may be imposed, the amount that can be collected is too small to provide adequate public services. In many of these states, the tax take per thousand dollars of personal income is a heavy one. Yet though a high *proportion* of aggregate income is taken in taxes, nevertheless, the taxpayers get little for their money. This is true because the whole state is poor. The result is poor schools and a generally low standard of public services despite the high tax take as a per cent of aggregate personal income.

Some northern states fall considerably below their northern neighboring states in public-service standards, and this is typically due to a relatively low ratio of tax revenues to aggregate personal income. Their fiscal problems arise not because they are poor but because their tax levels are low by northern standards. This is notably true for example of a tier of large industrial states— Illinois, Indiana, Ohio, and Pennsylvania. In terms of per capita expenditures (state and local) Illinois ranks thirtieth, Ohio, thirty-first, Indiana, thirty-third, and Pennsylvania, thirty-seventh [2]—in other words at the very bottom of the list of some thirty-five of the richer states of the Union. In terms of tax effort measured as ratio of revenues per thousand dollars of personal income, Pennsylvania ranks thirty-ninth among all the states of the Union; Indiana, fortieth; Illinois, forty-third; and Ohio, forty-seventh. Obviously these states are not excessively hard pressed by tax burdens relative to the country as a whole.

Basically, the question of the weight of the tax burden reduces to the matter of social values. Do we prize good public schools more than expensive "tail fins"? Recently Detroit, Michigan, held an election in which the citizens of this fifth largest city in the United States voted on a millage tax and a bond issue to provide funds for school expansion commensurate with a rapidly growing school population. All leaders in the community—business, labor, the churches, parent-teachers associations, the League of Women Voters, the newspapers—supported the tax increase and the proposed bond issue. Still, the tax and the bond issue were heavily voted down. Yet the average citizen may well have spent as much or more on his luxury automobile (amortization of the purchase price, interest, insurance, repairs, and operating expenses) as his aggregate state and local taxes. Indeed it is estimated that Americans spend more per year on automobiles than all state and local taxes put together.

Not only is the *average* tax burden relatively light in these four large industrial states; it is also regressive. None of these rich industrial states have an income tax. And so far as the country as a whole is concerned, although well over half of the states do have an income tax, still as an over-all average, state and local taxes, including all kinds of taxes, appear to be seriously regressive, as the accompanying table discloses. It may be added that, even at the federal level, the tax structure, including all federal taxes, does not really begin to become progressive until we reach the $15,000 income level.

---

[2] See James A. Maxwell, *Tax Credits and Intergovernmental Fiscal Relations.* Also see *A Staff Report, Measures of State and Local Fiscal Capacity and Tax Effort,* The Advisory Commission on Intergovernmental Relations, October, 1962.

Industry, so it is argued, tends to locate in states with low tax rates. The fear of competition tends to make legislatures reluctant to raise taxes. But as we have seen, low tax rates also yield low standards of public services. Families will find little inducement to locate in states where schools, hospitals, and municipal services of all kinds are below generally prevailing standards.

Estimated Tax Rates by Income Levels, 1958 [3]

Income	State and Local Taxes	Federal Taxes
Under $2,000	12.6%	15.7%
2,000–3,999	10.4	15.9
4,000–5,999	9.5	16.4
6,000–7,999	8.5	17.2
8,000–9,999	7.8	16.2
10,000–14,999	6.9	17.2
15,000 and over	6.1	29.8
All Classes	8.2	19.2

From the standpoint of industrial competition, however, we may be moving into a new era. Industry may increasingly be more interested in high standards of public services, in high standards of education, etc., than in low tax rates. One observes a growing number of advertisements by state development offices in which it is not the low tax rate that is played up; rather it is the alleged high quality of public education, municipal services, housing, hospital facilities, etc. Today, industry wants high school and college graduates, engineers, skilled technicians, and highly trained scientists. The U.S. Chamber of Commerce has alerted its local membership to do what they can to help reduce the percentage of ninth graders who drop out of school. We may well be moving into a period in which the high standards of public services argument may more and more take precedence over the low tax rate argument as far as state competition for industry is concerned.

Local governments often vote down bond issues for schools, sewage disposal, hospitals, and other urgently needed capital

[3] George A. Bishop, "The Tax Burden by Income Class, 1958," *National Tax Journal*, March, 1961.

facilities. Heated political arguments are concerned with the legit-
imacy of financing such improvements on the "pay-as-you-use"
principle. Sometimes local governments are confronted with legal
restraints. Often there is public apathy or fear of debt. Some local
governments may indeed be confronted with real limits, not
simply imaginary ones. Yet most readers will probably be sur-
prised to learn that the ratio of local debt to gross national product was 9 per cent in 1880, again in 1902, 10.9 per cent in 1913, and
only 10.2 per cent in 1960.[4] On a "pay-as-you-use" basis there is
far more room for sorely needed state and local expenditures than
current practice permits.

Of all our five "dynamic" factors making for an expanding
economy—three spontaneous and two discretionary—state and
local outlays have in fact ranked high during the last fifteen years.
Indeed, this is the only factor that has given the economy an
equally strong push in both 1948–56 and again in 1956–63. In
the latter period, state and local outlays performed the best of all,
exceeding by $3 billion the federal contribution. As far as *in-
creases* in outlays are concerned, state and local governments out-
distance private investment increases by sixfold. There is reason
to believe that state and local governments will continue to per-
form reasonably well within the severe limits of operation, but it
is scarcely plausible to assume that the record will outdo past
performance. If we are going to pull out of our semistagnation, we
shall have to look elsewhere.

Future Prospects

As far as can be learned, nobody believes that consumers'
durables can play the preponderant role which they did in 1948–
56. The volume of sales will remain high and it will grow, but the
growth will be a relatively modest one. Merely to hold its own
at a $50 billion per year level is no small achievement in a market
already well supplied. Henceforth, replacement will necessarily
be by far the major outlet.

With respect to defense, we must continue to hope that the
international situation will permit a cutback in defense expendi-

[4] *State Constitutional and Statutory Restrictions on Local Government Debt,*
Advisory Commission in International Relations, September, 1961, p. 18.

tures. Where would this leave us? A big tax cut—bigger than the cut in defense outlay—would be needed, as we know from the "balanced-budget theorem." We should need a drastic tax cut, or a large increase in civilian expenditures, or both.

This would put us severely to the test. Are we prepared to push forward with a full-employment program? Whether we take the increased civilian government expenditure route or the drastic tax cut, or both, large deficits will be incurred. This is true, at least unless a new technical revolution involving a vast release of "spontaneous" expansionist forces should suddenly loom up over the horizon.

Has Fiscal Policy Proved Itself Ineffective?

Critics of fiscal policy often say that postwar experience shows that it is relatively ineffective. Look at the huge postwar budgets, and yet we have semistagnation! What is wrong? To this there are at least two answers. The first has to do with the tax structure and with saving and investment. We have immunized the economy against the effectiveness of large budgets by a tax-rate structure so high that over-all cash budget surpluses begin to choke off recovery long before full employment is reached. Such restraint would indeed be fine if private investment were strong enough to swallow up the flow of both public and private saving generated at full employment.

This country is demonstrably a high-savings economy. As has been mentioned earlier, it generates an enormous volume of saving at high levels of employment—depreciation allowances, corporate retained earnings, pension funds, life and health insurance reserves, savings deposits, mutual funds, and large latent federal surpluses. No society can maintain its *current* achieved level of income unless all these savings funds can find borrowers—business borrowers, consumer borrowers, and government borrowers. If borrowers cannot be found, the potential savings go to waste and income declines. More than that, in a growing society, borrowing must exceed the funds offered by lenders; investment must exceed saving, or the economy cannot grow. To buy the larger product that will be produced "tomorrow" requires the spending not merely of the whole of today's income (including finding sufficient borrowers to take up all current savings). Credit expansion and new debt obligations also are needed to supplement current income sufficiently to take up tomorrow's *enlarged* output.

Viewed from the standpoint of the size of our GNP and our growth requirements, we need in this country a scale of borrowing considerably in excess of that recently experienced. Business, particularly since 1957, has borrowed too little, partly because of its own huge internal sources of funds, partly because for more than a decade, we have been building up a gigantic capacity of plant and equipment, partly because consumer demand has been shifting into services (an area in which the capital-output ratio is comparatively low), and partly because consumer demand has not been growing fast enough (the vicious circle) to induce a growing rate of investment. Consumers and state and local governments are perhaps borrowing as much as can be expected. So we are left with the federal government. The federal government has borrowed only a negligible amount in the postwar period. The federal debt in relation to GNP has fallen to half of the 1947 level. In the only terms that can have any real meaning, namely, the relation of debt to the size of the economy, the federal debt has been shrinking at a rapid—too rapid—rate. This was quite all right so long as business plus state and local governments were taking up the savings flow, as was roughly the case until 1957. And should technology open up vast new private investment outlets in the future, the "debt shrinking process" could be resumed. But when this is not the case, federal government borrowing is not only in order, but becomes a necessary condition for growth and expansion.

And now we give the second answer to the allegation that fiscal policy has not been able to turn the trick. The point that needs to be pressed home is this: growth and expansion cannot be achieved merely by maintaining current high levels of government expenditures (no matter how high) plus business outlays in investment. Growth requires *increases* of expenditures. Consumers, we know, will respond as far as their personal incomes grow together with some moderate trend growth in consumer credit. But the primary forward push must come from business investment and government outlays. So long as the business forward thrust was strong, as in the period 1948–56, so long as the international situation (defense) supplied a spontaneous outlet—just so long was there no great need for much deliberate or discretionary action. From 1957 on, the situation changed. The "spontaneous forces," though weaker, are by no means inconsiderable. They remain the basis for continued "high-level" stagnation with moderate growth. We continue to move forward to so-called record levels, but unemployment is rising and our rates of growth are too low. Deliberate policy has not been strong enough to get us back onto our normal growth trend.

Those who despair of deliberate policy are looking for some renewal of spontaneous forces. Some eagerly look forward to the household upsurge that is expected in the late sixties. We should not underestimate its importance, but we need a good empirical study of its probable impact. It has been suggested that any significant increase in spending will come some five years after the formation of new households. Two adults may continue to live on a restricted level saving up for the future. As the family grows, more space will eventually be needed. A secure job backed by some years' savings will justify some consumer debt for household equipment and a house. If this delayed spending theory is correct, the happy emergence of a new spontaneous factor will be pushed forward into the seventies.

Space. This will no doubt help to spur government spending, perhaps without much acrimonious debate. Space has all the allurements. As pure sport, it vastly exceeds horse racing or professional football. And it surely offers large possibilities for scientific research and technology. Space can be counted on the plus side, not indeed in terms of our serious public needs, but in terms of sheer expansion.

One can, however, see a grand long-range urban renewal program as the one big hope. Here is something that should appeal to the pocketbook. It is said that, for every dollar of federal money, private investment outlets of five to seven dollars can confidently be expected. We are learning about so-called French-type planning—business and government both committed to a well-developed, dependable, long-range program.[5] Urban renewal could be a gold mine for business. It could probably be sold to the Congress. We shall indeed do something for education, hospitals, and other urgent public needs. But large-scale commitments in these areas are scarcely probable. Urban renewal, with its pocketbook appeal, presents really big expansionist possibilities.

We hear much about business "confidence." Often the term is barren of real content. A development program budget, with prior congressional sanctions and commitments, could spark a large volume of private investment. This could put real meaning into the word "confidence." Business could budget ahead based on commitments to carry through an orderly long-range program.

There is growing evidence that fiscal policy will fail to operate at maximum effectiveness unless geared to planned development programs. Public spending and tax cuts, let loose on their own, can indeed, via the multiplier and the accelerator, substantially raise the national income. But the process is indirect and may involve serious lags and leakages. Hitched to a planned program the induced effects can quickly take hold. Business can know rather exactly what its investment outlets will be over a term of years. It can plan ahead. A planned development program is not just a "shot in the arm." In such an undertaking, both the spontaneous and the discretionary factors are marshaled together in a joint government-business undertaking. We may perhaps safely predict that this kind of planning will more and more become the leading characteristic of modern capitalism as we move into the last decades of the twentieth century.

There remains the dreadful prospect that we shall not tackle at all adequately the gigantic task of rehabilitating the deteriorating segment of our society—the delinquent and unemployed teenagers, the workers displaced by automation, the racial groups suffering from discrimination, the 8.3 million adult functional illiterates, the 7.7 million recipients of relief.

In Victorian England, Disraeli once said: "England consists of two nations—the rich and the poor." So in America two nations

---

[5] For an excellent discussion of the role of spontaneous forces vs. deliberate policy in the United States, in contrast with Europe, see Edward S. Mason, "Presidential Address," *American Economic Review*, March, 1963.

are developing—affluent America and deteriorating America. The difference is this: In Disraeli's time, the rich constituted a very small per cent of the population; the poor, the great masses. With us, affluent America is a vast majority—perhaps 85 per cent; deteriorating America is only some 15 per cent, but the proportion is apparently growing.

This problem cannot be solved by mere expansion of the economy. Expansion toward full employment is indeed a necessary condition; but it is not a sufficient condition to cure this distressing problem. The deteriorating segment of our society can never be rehabilitated except by a gigantic program involving very large federal expenditures over many years. Minor efforts will be swamped by the cumulative deteriorating forces already at work. Dr. Conant's great book on *Slums and Suburbs* presents the magnitude of the problem—social dynamite in the midst of our complacent, affluent society.

Abraham Lincoln, who had strong convictions about the role of government, has often been misquoted as saying that "government should do for the people only what they cannot do for themselves." But this is not what he said. Instead his statement suggests a positive, active role of government. The correct quotation is as follows: "The legitimate object of government is to do for the people what needs to be done, but which they can not, by individual effort, do at all, or do so well for themselves." [6]

[6] See Roy P. Basler, ed., *The Collected Works of Abraham Lincoln.*

3 · The Full-Employment Surplus and the Tax Cut

The Latent Surplus

In view of the fact that more often than not we have been running deficits rather than surpluses in the conventional administrative budget, the reader may think it strange to open this chapter with a section on budget surpluses. At 92 per cent full employment we have typically been running deficits of around three billion dollars or so. Why then talk about surpluses?

The answer to this conundrum is as follows. Given a certain level of expenditures, and given a certain structure of tax rates, revenues will rise if perchance the economy should move into higher gear in response to some powerful spontaneous factor (new products, for example, which could inaugurate a burst of investment in plant and equipment). Public expenditures not having increased, it follows that the increased tax receipts will rapidly bring the budget into balance and eventually produce a surplus. If the tax rates are so high that a near balance is achieved at low employment levels, it follows that such a tax structure would produce an overflow of receipts if high employment levels were reached. It follows also that if spontaneous forces should drive the economy upward, the increasing tax bite would act as a restraint on the expansion.

There can be no question about the great educational value of the "Full Employment Surplus" analysis which the Council of

Economic Advisers presented in January, 1962.[1] It has contributed in no small measure to a better public understanding of the role of fiscal policy. The fiscal-program curve, and its relative stability over recent years, has helped to drive home the point that, in the absence of a yearly increase in expenditures, or alternatively, a yearly reduction in tax rates, our tax structure acts continuously as a brake upon the economy.[2] This brake could completely have stopped all growth had it not in fact been eased by an approximately $5–6 billion yearly increase in federal expenditures (national income accounts) from 1956 to 1963.

This formulation of the impact of a given fiscal program upon expansion or restraint tells, of course, only a part of the story. There is, moreover, the danger, as is almost necessarily true of any proposition in so complicated a field of inquiry as economics, that quite erroneous conclusions may flow, seemingly inexorably, from the analysis. The formulation seems to suggest that if the "hurdle" of the restraint imposed by the latent full-employment surplus were removed by expenditure and tax policies, this in and of itself would ensure full employment. The analysis could indeed suggest that the concept of a "balanced budget" *per se* remains as an appropriate goal of national economic policy.[3] In short, it seems to suggest that a fiscal program which would produce a balanced budget at full employment would more or less *automatically* ensure a full-employment GNP.

I propose to incorporate the full-employment surplus within the broader pattern of the saving-investment problem. As a first step in this direction, Figure 3 includes, along with the latent budget surplus, the induced increments of private saving which emerge as full employment is approached. The full-employment surplus schedule by itself *alone* contributes little toward an understanding of the factors that determine whether the GNP is high or low. Within the framework of the saving-investment analysis, however, it supplies an important element, namely the contribu-

---

[1] *Economic Report of the President,* pp. 78–81.
[2] This general approach has for many years been the central thesis of the Committee for Economic Development.
[3] Similarly, those who advocate the adoption of a capital budget (desirable in itself as good accounting procedure) appear at times to suggest that it be made the basis for fiscal policy decisions.

tion of the federal government (tax rates and expenditures being given) to aggregate gross saving.[4]

Figure 3 shows the increments of (a) federal government saving and (b) private saving above (or below) the point at which

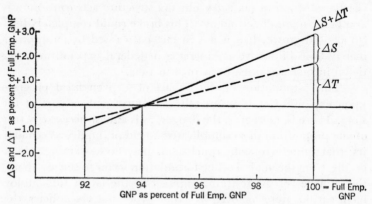

FIGURE 3. *The Latent Budget Surplus*

federal government net saving is *zero,* i.e., the budget is in balance, i.e., $T = G$.[5] Let us call this point the "zero" point. The govern-

---

[4] Gross saving equals (a) gross *private* saving, plus (b) government net saving (or dissaving). Gross saving (public and private), *ex post,* will always equal gross private investment. It follows that gross *private* saving will not equal gross private investment except in the special case when government net saving is zero (i.e., when the budget is in balance). See the precise definitions given below.

[5] The reader should note carefully the somewhat arbitrary definitions here used for the different symbols. "G" stands for federal government expenditures (national income accounts, which include transfer payments). "I" stands for gross private investment, including net exports of goods and services. "S" stands for gross *private* saving, including, be it noted, the net saving (or dissaving) of state and local governments but *not* including the net saving (or dissaving) of the federal government. "T" stands for the tax and other receipts (national income accounts) of the federal government, including the trust funds. $(T - G) =$ federal net saving.

It should be noted that, in line with these definitions, $GNP - (I + G)$ is *not* equal to private consumption. Rather $GNP - (I + G)$, as here used is equal to private consumption, plus state and local expenditures (i.e., community consumption), less federal transfers to the public and to state and local bodies. In short, $GNP - (I + G)$ is equal to "self-financed personal consumption plus self-financed state and local expenditures."

ment surplus plus the private saving differential will tell us how much gross private investment must rise above the "zero" point level in order to reach full employment via the route of an investment boom. Similarly, at the left of the "zero" point, one sees how far investment must fall to drive the GNP down sufficiently to produce the indicated government deficit and the negative private saving differential.

Figure 3, although schematic and not intended to be accurate, does fairly well disclose the *average* situation for the four semistagnant years 1958–61, and it fits almost exactly the actual data for the year 1961. For the four-year period as a whole, the economy *averaged* about 8 per cent below full employment. At this level of GNP, the average federal deficit (national income accounts) was about $3 billion, and the negative private saving differential was about $2 billion. Had full employment been reached, however, an average federal surplus of $9 would have appeared, together with a positive private saving differential of about $6 billion. From the low point to the high point, the aggregate *increase* in saving (public and private) would have been about $20 billion; hence, to reach full employment via the investment route would have required an *increase* in gross private investment of around $20 billion.

The full-employment surplus (when supplemented by the private saving differentials) does indeed provide one of the basic factors needed for income determination. Still this incremental type of analysis is not quite adequate. A clearer picture will emerge if we consider the role of the G and T schedules as aggregates in relation to the I and S schedules.

The (S + T) Schedule

The relation of the (S + T) schedule to GNP is shown in Figure 4. Also, the T schedule is shown separately, and the S schedule is represented by the area between the (S + T) curve and the T curve. The nine observations cover the period 1954–62—a period in which tax *rates* remained for the most part fairly stable. The regression lines fitted to these observations disclose a stable relation, year after year. For any given increase in GNP, private

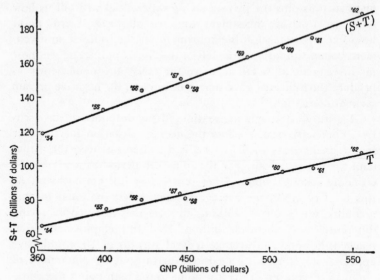

FIGURE 4. *The Relation of the (S + T) Schedule to GNP*

saving and federal receipts rose, as indicated, in a fairly dependable manner as revealed by the slope of the curves. The slope of the T schedule $\left(\dfrac{\triangle T}{\triangle GNP}\right)$ was 0.23; that of the (S + T) schedule $\left[\dfrac{\triangle(S + T)}{\triangle GNP}\right]$ was 0.38, which gives the S schedule slope a value of 0.15.

For convenience, in what follows, let us use round figures (nine observations are in any event not enough to justify too great refinements). Thus we shall assume that the slope for the T schedule was 0.25, and for the (S + T) schedule 0.40. The slope for the T schedule tells us that, for every $100 increase in GNP, approximately $25 was captured by the federal government in the national income account receipts. Only a part of this, however, would show up in the administrative budget receipts, the rest going to the trust funds. The slope of the (S + T) schedule tells us that we might normally assume a multiplier (k) of approximately 2.5.

The slope of the T schedule for the period covered was tilted up somewhat (upward shifts in the schedule) by reason of the built-in increases in social security tax rates. This development was, however, offset more or less by opposite tendencies that tended to flatten the slope of the T schedule. Corporate profits ran pretty much on a flat plateau, owing partly to the slow rate of growth of the economy, and partly to the exceptionally rapid rise in depreciation allowances from $11.8 billion in 1953 to $26.2 billion in 1961. These factors had the effect of narrowing the profit margin and so tended to hold back normal increases in corporate income taxes.

Given the T and S schedule, the actual level of GNP will depend upon the level of gross private investment and government outlays. Without embarking upon the difficult problem of interdependence, we shall here assume that I and G are in large measure autonomously determined. Investment outlays and government expenditures are the result of decisions made by men of affairs—businessmen and government officials—based on innumerable and highly complicated matters, among which exogenous factors play a major but not exclusive role.

Figure 5 shows the intersection of the (I + G) schedule with

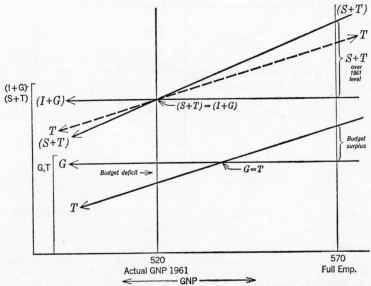

FIGURE 5. *The Intersection of the (I + G) Schedule with the (S + G) Schedule*

the (S + T) schedule.[6] The data are derived from the calendar year 1961. The equilibrium level of GNP settled at $520 billion. Broadly speaking, the chart presents substantially the same picture as Figure 3. Here, however, the G and T schedules are placed against the background of the over-all savings-investment problem.

By shifting any one (or more) of the four schedules, we can readily trace the impact upon the GNP and upon government deficits and surpluses. In particular let us experiment a bit with fiscal policy shifts designed to achieve fuller employment. We shall consider two approaches to this problem: Case A, a $10 billion increase in federal outlays, and Case B, a $10 billion cut in taxes. The results are shown in Figures 6 and 7. In view of past relationships, based, however, on an inadequate number of observations, these results may perhaps be regarded as reasonably plausible, though certainly a long way from being dependable or predictable.

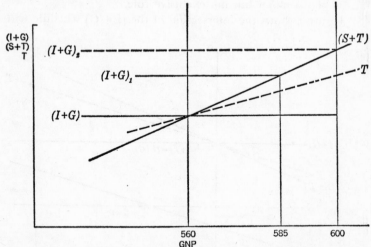

FIGURE 6. *Case A: A Ten-Billion-Dollar Increase in the (I + G) Schedule*

[6] Without going into unnecessary detail, it may simply be remarked here that crossing the (I + G) curve with the (T + S) curve is merely an expansion of the familiar crossing of the I and S curves to determine the level of GNP.

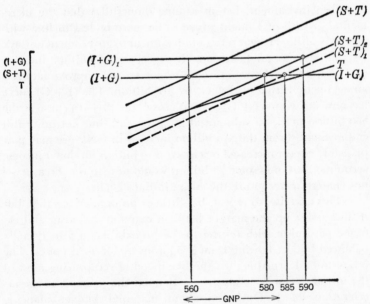

FIGURE 7. *Case B: A Ten-Billion-Dollar Reduction in the (S + T) Schedule*

A Ten-billion Increase in Expenditures

Case A: Starting from a GNP of $560 billion (approximately that of 1962), we introduce an increase in government expenditures. As a first approximation, we shift the $(I + G)$ schedule up by $10 billion to become $(I + G)_1$. The $(I + G)_1$ curve now crosses the $(S + T)$ curve at the $585 billion GNP level, an increase of $25 billion (the multiplier, as we have seen, being 2.5). In accordance with the slope of the T schedule, such an increase in GNP should raise the national income accounts receipts by $6.25 billion. Of this, only some 80 per cent would flow into the Treasury, the rest going into the trust funds. Thus the Treasury might recapture only $5 billion of the $10 billion deficit initially created by the increased expenditures.

An increase of $25 billion in GNP, however, could certainly be expected to have some induced effect (the acceleration principle) on investment. Let us assume (hopefully) that the incremental growth of I might prove to be more or less in line with the fairly normal recent ratios of investment to government outlays. On this basis, we might reasonably expect say a $6 billion increase in "I." Accordingly, we move on to our second approximation—an aggregate lifting of $(I + G)$ by $16 billion. The $(I + G)$ curve has now shifted to $(I + G)_2$, and it crosses the $(S + T)$ curve at the 600 billion mark—a substantial improvement, but not quite full employment. From the $40 billion increase in GNP, we may now plausibly expect increased receipts of $10 billion (national income accounts). But only some $8 billion would flow to the Treasury—not enough to recapture the entire initial deficit.

This exercise, to repeat, has little or no predictive value, but it does point up the margin between extreme optimism and extreme pessimism with respect to the probability of a marginally balanced budget flowing from a vigorous use of fiscal policy. The lesson to be learned is this: the likelihood of recapturing most of the initial deficit depends primarily upon the strength of the acceleration effect. Optimism about marginal budget-balancing must rest basically upon faith in the stimulating effect of expansionist fiscal policy upon the inducement to invest.

A Ten-billion Cut in Taxes

Consider next Case B—a tax cut—as shown in Figure 7. As a first approximation, we assume a downward shift in the $(S + T)$ schedule to $(S + T)_1$. This implies an increase in GNP of $25 billion to $585 billion. But this first approximation is clearly not defensible because not all of the tax relief will be spent—a part will be saved, possibly $2 billion. This shifts the $(S + T)$ curve up, as a second approximation, to $(S + T)_2$ and the GNP now shrinks from $585 billion to $580 billion. So far we have assumed no acceleration effect. Since the tax cut boost has now been cut down to $8 billion (after taking account of the induced increase in saving), we can expect a somewhat smaller acceleration effect than that assumed in Case A, say, perhaps a $4 billion increase in I. The $(I + G)$ curve now shifts, as a third approximation to $(I + G)_1$ and crosses the $(S + T)_2$ curve at the $590 billion GNP level. In the final analysis, then, GNP is lifted by $30 billion, and the "super-multiplier" applied to the $10 billion tax cut turns out to be only 3. A $30 billion increase in GNP suggests recovery of $7.5 billion in receipts of which some $6 billion would flow to the Treasury. This would leave a net marginal deficit of some $4 billion.

Transitory vs. Permanent Deficits

It has often been suggested that a tax cut might well induce so large an increase in GNP that the recaptured revenues could eventually more than offset the initial deficit. Thus President Kennedy, in his speech to the New York Economic Club on December 14, 1962, alluded to a "temporary deficit of transition, resulting from a tax cut designed to boost the economy, increase tax revenue and achieve a future budget surplus."

This eventuality is certainly not impossible. The foregoing analysis, however, helps us to keep our feet on the ground. In the case of a tax cut, even a marginally balanced budget (let alone a surplus) could scarcely be expected from a *normally* strong acceleration effect. But, if latent *autonomous* forces (advances in technology, etc.) have been accumulating—lying dormant and not yet having found corporeal expression in new investment—then the stimulus of a tax cut might well open the door to the full force of these exogenous expansionist factors. The increased spending, directly flowing from the tax cut, plus the normal acceleration effect, plus the release of latent autonomous forces, could indeed, under a combination of favorable circumstances, raise the GNP to the point suggested by the President.[7] More probably, in the usual case, we should have to settle for a continuing deficit equal to, say, a quarter or a third of the initial tax cut.

The events of the last fifteen years, including, it should be noted, the eight years of the Eisenhower Administration, reaffirm the long-standing lesson of history that growth requires an increase in money, credit, and debt. And in the public-private economy of today, a well-balanced growth suggests an increase of debt at all levels—business debt, consumer debt, state and local debt,

---

[7] Especially in the first year or two of a vigorous upturn, revenues might rise sharply. Thus the spurt from 1954 to 1955 boosted the budget receipts of fiscal 1956 mainly as a result of the temporary sharp rise in corporate profits.

and federal debt. History shows that aggregate debt tends to rise more or less in direct proportion to increases in GNP, or in other words, the ratio of aggregate debt to GNP tends to remain fairly constant. Past relationships indicate that a growth in GNP of $25 billion per year requires approximately an increase in aggregate debt of about $40 billion to $45 billion per year. Since the federal government contributes about 20 per cent of the aggregate flow of GNP, it is not unreasonable to suppose that the government might assume about $8 billion to $10 billion of the per annum aggregate increase in debt. A major cause of the sluggish rise in GNP in recent years is our failure to permit a balanced expansion in the federal debt via either tax cuts or greater increases in federal expenditures.

Booming investment outlets could indeed swallow up budget surpluses and marginal increases in private saving and thereby produce both full employment and a balanced or even an over-balanced budget. Private investment and private debt, if large enough, could conceivably carry the load. So the question arises why in fact this has not occurred in the post-Korean years. One might indeed well have expected overflowing private investment, stimulated as it has been by the huge cold war military contracts and the rapid growth of population. Military hardware requires heavy investment in plant and equipment. And urbanization, in contrast with rural living, requires a vast investment overhead. Still private investment has languished. Why?

The Problem of Investment Outlets

Many reasons have been assigned for the recent poor investment record in the United States. Among other things, it has been suggested that the growth of oligopoly is one reason for the tendency of investment to lag under modern conditions. Oligopolies, it is said, confronted with a downward-sloping demand curve, tend to limit their investment within the bounds of a restricted market, whereas a single competitor among many in a competitive situation is confronted with a horizontal demand curve, and therefore (for him) a limitless market and, as he sees it, unbounded investment opportunities.[8] As a long-run trend this contention may have

---

[8] See P. Sylos-Labini, *Oligopoly and Technical Progress*, Harvard University Press, 1962.

merit. But in the period since 1957 what seems most impressive in comparing the sluggishness of investment in the United States with the buoyancy of investment in western Europe is the fact that, with us, the demand for consumers' durables has remained on a stagnant plateau, whereas in Europe, with their rapidly rising standard of living, the market in consumers' durables is only now opening up in a big way. With respect to durables, Europe is currently very much where we were back in the booming twenties. This difference in our respective situations accounts in no small measure for the sluggish investment here and the booming investment there.

In the United States, the biggest growth sector is "services." But we have already noted a difficulty: services require less capital investment per dollar unit of output than consumers' durables. The capital-output ratio is lower. Moreover, the service area, fast-growing as it is, is not growing fast enough to absorb the unemployed. Adequate growth in the service area requires large government outlays. If education, schools, hospitals, medical schools, nursing schools, nursing homes, technical training and retraining centers, urban mass transit systems, water resources, river antipollution projects, parks, open sites for recreation, civic cultural centers, and even such traditional functions as police protection and well-paved streets were given sufficient support to bring the public sector up to the best standards of the private sector—if these things were done, the service area would grow by leaps and bounds and these public outlays would in turn provide a wide range of outlays for private investment. A growing demand for education will induce no private investment unless school bonds are voted to provide schools. In contrast, a growing demand for consumers' durables *automatically* opens up private investment outlays.

Our modern scarcities are not in consumers' durables; they are in the area of services associated with (a) the conglomeration of vast populations in urban communities, (b) the skills required by an advanced technology, (c) the cultural needs and aspirations of high community living standards.

Private investment outlets have, of course, not dried up by any means. From 1957 to 1962 inclusive, gross private investment amounted in the aggregate to around $425 billion or about $70 billion per year. This is not a bad record but it is not good enough.

The current tax-cut proposal is essentially an effort to end our high-level stagnation by lifting private investment to higher levels. This can be done, it is hoped, by easing the tax burdens on corporations and by the impact of higher consumer demand (the acceleration effect) on private investment. Yet without the stimulus of substantially larger government expenditures, an adequate increase in investment may not occur. A tax cut will help, but it does not meet squarely the urgent needs imposed by the service-oriented economy of a highly urbanized society.

Nevertheless, there can be no doubt that our tax structure is repressive and a tax cut is desirable.[9] But alone, it will not do the job, nor does it measure up to the social-priorities test of the best allocation of resources. A tax cut, however, is clearly in line with current social values, and this cannot be overlooked in a political democracy. Indeed, it is doubtful whether the public-sector approach can ever be fully accepted until we have employed to the limit the "market" approach, namely, pushing private expenditures to a far deeper saturation point than has so far been reached. The disparity between the marginal utility of the pay-envelope dollar and the marginal utility of the public-expenditure dollar has to be widened a good deal more before it becomes crystal clear that our modern scarcities lie in the public sector. In the meantime, the pressure of ever-present public wants will push us year by year, both at the state and federal level, into increased, though seriously inadequate, public expenditures.[10]

To sum up, the whole thing can be put in a nutshell: In the United States the (S + T) schedule is too high and the (I + G) schedule is too low.

One final brief comment about the first horn of our dilemma –the (S + T) function. In the previous section, the main emphasis

---

[9] See the author's letter to *The New York Times*, May 27, 1962, and Alvin H. Hansen, "A Permanent Tax Cut Now," *Challenge*, October, 1962.

[10] Europe, especially on the Continent, presents not only a more favorable situation with respect to private investment as just indicated, but also a more favorable climate, from the standpoint of social psychology and social values, for making the necessary adjustments to the demands of a "service" economy. This is true because there government has traditionally been accepted as the natural instrument to foster the needs of an advanced society in its effort to meet the demands of highly urbanized and culturally rich communities.

has been placed on the T schedule. What about the S schedule? A difficult question. It is rather easy to agree on tax policy. It is not so easy to agree on policy with respect to saving. Is the saving schedule too high or too low? On this there will be wide differences of opinion. In my analysis of secular stagnation made a generation ago, I invariably concentrated on inadequate investment outlets. It was not argued that the propensity to save had been rising secularly; on the contrary, it was held that the propensity to save had remained approximately stable. The analysis ran in terms of investment, not in terms of saving. One may suspect that again today our trouble is inadequate investment, not too high a propensity to save. Growth demands a high rate of investment public and private, and this necessarily implies a high rate of saving.

It is, however, quite possible that recent institutional changes are working in the direction of pushing the S schedule upward. In this connection, note may be taken of the growth of pension funds, of mutual investment funds, of building and loan associations, of time and savings deposits, of accelerated depreciation allowances, of low break-even points in oligopolistic industries, and finally the upward-tilting impact on the S schedule of the built-in stabilizers. Whether the S schedule has, on balance, in recent times been trending up or down is by no means altogether clear. Gross private saving amounted to 15.0 per cent of GNP in the high-employment year 1929. It *averaged* 15.3 per cent of GNP in the five relatively low-employment years 1957–61 inclusive.[11] This occurred although the tax take was far higher in 1957–61 than in 1929. In a sluggish economy, we might have expected the realized private savings to have fallen even though the saving-schedule may have risen. Empirical research into *ex post* saving, considered by itself alone, can mislead us.

Savings-Investment 1956–63

Throughout this period, the latent federal surplus, plus the potential increase in private saving which a full-employment in-

---

[11] Given the same propensity to save, it is clear that a smaller amount (a smaller ratio of saving to GNP) will be saved in low-employment years. Since in fact a slightly larger proportion was saved in the low-income years than in the highly prosperous year 1929, it appears that the saving function may have shifted slightly upward.

come would produce, amounted on the average to around $20 billion. This means that it would have required a sharp increase in private investment to reach full employment via the investment route. With large excess capacity following the postwar investment spurt of 1955–56, this was not attainable.

But what about federal expenditures? Throughout the 1956–63 period (1960 omitted) the administrative budget expenditures increased by $14.1 billion (1956–59) under Eisenhower and by $12.8 billion (1961–63) under Kennedy. Cash payments (1960 omitted) increased by around $7.5 billion per year (Eisenhower) to about $8.5 per year (Kennedy).

These expenditure increases were just about enough to offset the potential increase in revenue automatically induced by growth. This left the saving-investment problem unchanged. The economy throughout the period hovered at 92 per cent of full employment. A society with a rapidly growing population and large increases in productivity must run fast to remain in the same place.

In fiscal 1960, President Eisenhower made a desperate effort to balance the budget. Instead of the average per annum $5 billion increase in the administrative budget expenditures, the 1960 budget was cut back by nearly $4 billion. This action contributed to cutting short a recovery after only 25 months of advance.

In a somewhat comparable stage in the recovery movement, President Kennedy proposed for fiscal 1964 an increase in the administrative budget of $4.5 billion, which, however, was perhaps about $1.5 billion short of the figure needed merely to offset automatic revenue increases. Private investment, an equally potent offset, was, however, beginning to respond to the 1962 investment tax credit and to the new depreciation guidelines. There was, moreover, the prospect of a proposed tax cut to be spread over two or three years. Business prospects seemed to offer the hope that the periodically recurring recession due in 1963–64 might be avoided. Indeed, one might propose a question for business-cycle analysts to speculate about: how far a dependable per annum increase in federal expenditures of, say, $6 billion [12]

---

[12] An increase of this magnitude in the years immediately ahead would not fully meet the growing needs in the public sector.

(plus the recently experienced per annum increase of about $4 billion in state and local expenditures) might prevent recessions altogether. Of course the absolute expenditure increase would need to be adjusted upward, as time goes on, to the requirements of growth. This, of course, would not imply a *uniform* rate of growth in GNP each year, but only the prevention of a downturn. This tentative (and optimistic) conclusion would of course become more plausible if a steadily rising expenditure policy were supported by effective *counter-cyclical* tax and monetary policies.

Some reader may feel that my accelerator, as used in this chapter, is too small. One must bear in mind, however, that the accelerator is much smaller than the marginal capital-output ratio. The net addition to capital stock in any period consists partly of autonomous investment and partly of induced investment. The accelerator measures the ratio of *induced* investment to the increment of output.

There is moreover the additional fact that the accelerator will be small whenever there is large unused capacity.

4 · Growth Trends and the Business Cycle

In the postwar period too much attention has been devoted merely to the *range* of fluctuations without paying attention to the potential growth trend. The range of the fluctuation of the cycle may be quite narrow while at the same time the spread between the *actual* output (GNP in real terms) and the potential growth trend may be large and perhaps increasing. Much has been said about the mildness of a recession (a few percentage points below the previous peak), and subsequently about recovery "records" even though these so-called "records" were moving farther and farther away from the growth trend that a dynamic society could be expected to achieve.

Some economists, however, have sought to show that the dynamic forces at work producing the recovery phase of the cycle are precisely the growth factors, and that moreover the limits of the potential growth trend may play an important restraining effect on the boom.

Hicks on Growth and the Cycle

In his article, "Mr. Harrod's Dynamic Theory" (*Economics,* May, 1949) and in *The Trade Cycle,* Hicks develops a cycle theory based on the combination of a continuing growth (with occasional spurts) of autonomous investment together with the multiplier and acceleration effect of such movements upon aggregate investment, and through investment in turn upon aggregate output.

The analysis can perhaps best be followed by reference to Figure 8.

I_A represents a steady growth of autonomous investment in a dynamic society continuously making progress in technology. kaI_A represents the magnified investment resulting from the ever-growing autonomous investment. The fact that autonomous in-

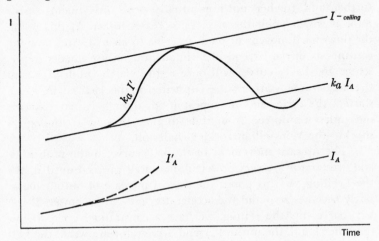

FIGURE 8. *Hicks' Theory of the Cycle*

vestment is growing causes, via the multiplier, an increase in consumption outlays, and this in turn, via the accelerator, causes a rise in aggregate investment represented by the curve kaI_A. Associated with this investment curve is a level of national income (not shown on the chart) commensurate with the level of aggregate investment represented by kaI_A.

I'_A represents a spurt of autonomous investment, such as might develop from the introduction of an exceptionally important new technique. It is the Wicksellian push to the rocking chair. Indeed Hicks' theory is a combination of Wicksell's rocking chair plus the continuous *growth* of autonomous investment. The autonomous investment *spurt* will swerve the curve off its trend course, driving it up toward the I-ceiling. The I-ceiling represents the full-capacity utilization of the industries producing capital goods. Associated with this full-capacity investment ceiling, we assume a full-employment aggregate output (also not shown on the chart). As the kaI' curve moves toward the I-ceiling, the rate of *increase* of output will begin to decline. As soon as this happens, the accelerator begins to go into reverse, forcing a downward movement of the kaI' curve. The interaction of the accelerator and the multiplier will drive the kaI' curve down further and further until eventually gross investment equals zero, at which point the accelerator ceases to act. At this point, the downward movement tends to come to an end. And now the continuous upward trend of technological improvements (represented by the I_A curve) will once again, via the multiplier and the accelerator, start another upswing of the kaI' curve. Once started, the cycle tends to repeat itself, though it may dampen out unless reinforced from time to time by new technological shocks—the Wicksellian rocking-chair jolt.

The upward movement of the kaI' curve, if the multiplier and accelerator are very powerful, may well proceed until it hits the I-ceiling. At this point, the rate of increase of output necessarily becomes zero and the accelerator loses all its power. If the kaI' curve hits the ceiling, we have a constrained cycle. If, on the other hand, the multiplier and accelerator are weak, the kaI' curve will flatten out before the I-ceiling is reached. It flattens out because the *rate of increase* of output is weakened by reason of ever-growing bottlenecks—scarcities of production factors— long before the I-ceiling is reached. This Hicks calls the "free cycle." A powerful multiplier or accelerator, or both, may, however, despite bottlenecks, be sufficiently strong to drive the kaI' curve fully up to the I-ceiling. In either case, the slowing down of the rate of increase will throw the accelerator into reverse and start the downward movement.

Capital-output Ratio, Income-investment Ratio, and Autonomous Net Investment

$\frac{K}{O}$, or the "capital-output ratio," represents the average relation of the aggregate stock of capital (plant, equipment, and inventories) to output per annum. $\frac{\triangle K}{\triangle O}$ represents the "marginal capital-output ratio."

Given the state of technology, a certain stock of capital is optimally necessary to produce a given volume of output. If sales increase, entrepreneurs will need to expand their plant and equipment; or conversely, if expectations of sales justify expansion, a net addition to the stock of capital will make possible an increase in output. Bold entrepreneurs may push ahead and increase output capacity, step up their marketing drive, and sell the enlarged output. Thus the capital stock may grow *because* more plant and equipment are required to match the anticipated growing demand with a growing output. Here, the growing O induces an increase in K. Or again, a boldly expanded K will produce a large O. Whichever takes the lead, a capital-output adjustment process is always going on. This is the essence of the "capital adjustment theory" of the business cycle.

Historically, the capital-output ratio, $\frac{K}{O}$, has been remarkably stable—around 3/1. From about the eighteen-eighties to around 1920, the capital-output ratio was apparently rising somewhat; after 1920, we note a falling tendency. This doubtless reflects a change in technology. Inventions may be capital-saving, meaning relatively less capital per unit of output. Or an invention may be capital-using, meaning more capital per unit of output. But we should not forget that, barring a fall in the rate of interest, inventions must always be *labor-saving*, whether they are capital-saving or capital-using inventions. The progress of technology, broadly stated, means less labor per unit of output, taking the entire productive process into consideration. $\frac{K}{O}$ may remain constant, or the ratio may rise or fall, but however that may be, the stock of capital in relation to labor, $\frac{K}{L}$, has always risen historically, and so also has $\frac{O}{L}$. Were this not so, new investment in plant and equipment would not have been made.

Entrepreneurs will always be busily engaged making the appropriate adjustment of capital stock to output. In Figure 9, we represent this relationship in the curves labeled K and O. The two curves are tied together by the capital-output ratio, which we shall call "c." Thus $c = \dfrac{K}{O}$, or marginally, $c = \dfrac{\triangle K}{\triangle O}$.

The K and O have already been taken care of in what has been said earlier. Below the aggregate output line, O, we see a line labeled (I + G). This represents gross private domestic investment and federal government expenditures (national income accounts). In 1962, I was \$75 billion, and G was \$110 billion. For 1962, $\dfrac{GNP}{I + G}$ was equal to 3, and this ratio held, broadly speaking, with more or less variation, over the recent past. Gross private investment and federal outlays are the result of decision-making largely of an autonomous character. Given a set of institutions and behavior patterns of business firms and individuals, the volume of gross private saving can be regarded as a function

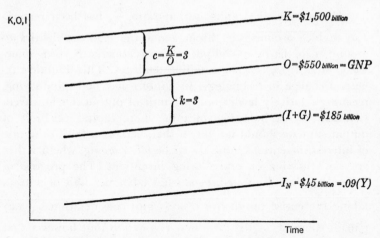

FIGURE 9. *Capital-Output Ratio, Income-Investment Ratio, and Autonomous Net Investment*

of GNP. And similarly, given a tax structure, the volume of tax receipts will depend upon the size of the GNP. Combining these two functions, we get a schedule, (T + S), showing the amount of taxes and private saving combined at various levels of GNP. The shape of this curve will give us the multiplier relation of (I + G) to GNP, i.e., k(I + G) = GNP.

The multiplier appears to be roughly around 2.5, as shown in Figure 4.

Finally we come to *net* investment, I_N. This, in recent years, has normally amounted to approximately 9 per cent of GNP, or recently around $45 billion. Now 9 per cent of GNP is about 3 per cent of the capital stock K. And if the capital stock grows by about 3 per cent per year, we can expect, from the relationship just indicated, that output, GNP, in real terms, will grow at about the same percentage rate. This at least would tend to hold so long as the ratio of $\frac{K}{O}$ remains about the same. It must be remembered, however, that $\frac{\triangle K}{\triangle O}$ will vary considerably over the cycle. Thus the growth of GNP from 1961 to 1962 was 5 per cent, not 3 per cent.

The Harrod-Domar Growth Equation

The Harrod-Domar equation for growth is $g = \frac{s}{c}$. "g" is the rate of growth; "s" is the ratio of net saving to aggregate income; and "c" is the capital-output ratio. A large s makes *possible* a high rate of investment and thus (if in fact the investment is made) a high rate of growth. A small c means that a relatively large output can be obtained from a given net addition to the capital stock. Thus the rate of growth is directly proportional to s and inversely proportional to c.

The actual figures for the United States, under normal conditions, are approximately as follows: $s = 0.09$, $c = 3$, and so $g = 0.03$, i.e., a 3 per cent rate of growth.

This simple equation raises more questions than it answers. First we must know whether the s ratio is a marginal or an average ratio of saving to income. If the marginal s is larger than the average s, then within the range of this marginal curve, aggregate saving, S, in relation to aggregate income, Y (i.e., $\frac{S}{Y}$) will be an increasing function of income. It follows from our equation ($gc = s$) that the rate of growth (g) will then also be an increasing function of income. From this, we conclude that, in these circumstances, a full-employment income will yield not only a *higher level* of income, but also a *higher rate of growth*.

This, however, would not be true in the event that the marginal s were always equal to the average s. For in this case the $\frac{S}{Y}$ would be a constant at all levels of income.[1] And if $\frac{S}{Y}$ were a constant at all levels of income, the same rate of growth would hold whether the economy were running along at full employment or considerably below full employment. It is of course theoretically possible that an economy utilizing 80 per cent of capacity could *grow* at exactly the same percentage *rate* as an economy utilizing 100 per cent of capacity. At any rate, we know that, in a cyclically fluctuating economy, $\frac{S}{Y}$ is lower in depression years than in full-employment years, and therefore a stable full-employment economy can experience a higher rate of growth than an economy which fluctuates.

In the case of a stable underemployment economy, the matter is not so clear. Perhaps here a favorable verdict, as far as the growth *rate* is concerned, would have to rely on faith that a full-employment economy tends to encourage not only a higher ratio of $\frac{S}{Y}$ but also offers a more favorable climate for technological progress.

This leads us to consider the role of c in the *rate* of growth. Here again c can be defined either in terms of a long-run average ratio of capital to output, $\frac{K}{O}$, or as a short-run marginal ratio, $\frac{\triangle K}{\triangle O}$. Over the long run, c apparently has remained fairly constant at around 3/1. The marginal c can, however, vary considerably up and down over the short run, especially in various phases of the business cycle. Now it could be possible that a full employment economy might show a different marginal c than an underemployment economy. Would the marginal c be higher or lower under conditions of full employment? Presumably it

---

[1] We assume that the $\frac{S}{Y}$ curve starts at point of origin.

would be lower. This would appear probable because, under the pressure of high employment, the capital stock would be used more intensively than at lower levels of employment. Thus as we move from low to high employment, the marginal c would tend to fall. On the other hand, it could be argued that the growing scarcity of labor, together with the concomitant rise in wage rates would tend to induce the substitution of machinery for labor; hence the marginal c might tend to rise.

If now the marginal c is high, the rate of growth will tend to be lower than would otherwise be the case; and conversely, if the marginal c is low, the rate of growth will tend to be greater. In some industries, the tendencies making for a high marginal c, as full employment is approached, may predominate over those making for a low marginal c, whereas in others the reverse may be the case. Theoretical analyses cannot give a clean-cut answer, and empirical research is as yet inconclusive. Taking account of both s and c, however, it is perhaps plausible to conclude that a full-employment economy is likely to experience not only the obvious advantage of a higher *level* of income, but also the less obvious probable achievement of a higher *rate of growth* than a slack economy. Yet it is theoretically conceivable that a less than full-employment society, although offering a lower current standard of living, might promise a higher growth rate. More likely, however, the opposite will be the case.

If marginal s is larger than average s, it follows that $\frac{S}{Y}$ is an increasing function of income. In this event, our growth equation cannot tell us what the rate of growth will be unless we already know what the income will be. But is there perhaps something inherent in the capital-output ratio which determines the level of income? This idea cannot altogether be dismissed, since the marginal capital-output ratio is certainly a function of changing technology. And a changing technology is a determinant of real income. An improving technique and a growing population open up investment outlets; and investment, via the multiplier and the accelerator, determines the level of output.

Changing techniques may be either capital-saving, thereby tending to reduce c, or they may be capital-using, thereby tending to increase the value of c. If c falls, the effect will be one thing in the short run and another thing in the long run. Or more precisely, the effect is one thing on the level of current aggregate demand and another on the productive power of a full-employment economy. On the level of current aggregate demand, a lower c is unfavorable, since a lower c opens up smaller investment outlets than a higher c. A lower c means a smaller acceleration effect. But a lower c also means a more efficient society and therefore a larger real income, provided always that full employment can somehow be achieved despite the diminished investment outlets. A lower c tends in the short run to make it more difficult, if reliance is placed upon spontaneous forces (and less on deliberate policy) to reach a full-employment aggregate demand. But it makes for a larger output potential if, indeed, full employment can be achieved.

It appears therefore evident that our growth equation, $g = \frac{s}{c}$, cannot tell us what the level of income will be. Instead we must look to the theory of income determination to find the level of income. And we need to know the level of income before we can know the value of s. Only then can the rate of growth be derived from our equation.

The theory of income determination is based on the following tools of analysis: (a) the marginal efficiency of capital schedule, (b) the consumption function, (c) the liquidity preference schedule, (d) the money supply.[2] In a dynamic society, the marginal efficiency schedule will always be in process of shifting up or to the right. This shift is primarily a function of technological innovations and growth in the labor force. Technology and growth of population (in terms both of quantity and quality) are the prime determinants of growth.

The Harrod-Domar growth equation can be a useful tool of analysis, but it can easily be misused. It has, in fact, been employed in planning programs for the development of economically backward countries in a far more rigid manner than is justified. The

---

[2] See also Alvin H. Hansen, *Guide to Keynes,* and, of course, Keynes, *General Theory of Employment, Interest and Money,* Harcourt, Brace, and World, 1936.

capital-output ratio varies from industry to industry, from country to country, and from one stage of economic development to another. It will be one thing if the planned program for development emphasizes heavy industry (steel, etc.) and quite a different thing if the planned program emphasizes education, agriculture, and population control. The capital-output ratio analysis tends almost inevitably to overemphasize brick and mortar and to underemphasize investment in human resources. In fact, the standard statistical measurements of capital-output ratios are based entirely on estimates of the accumulated stock of material capital goods. Yet fully as important, if indeed not more important, is the stock of human capital—knowledge, skill of all kinds.[3] Why was the Marshall aid program so effective whereas the Alliance for Progress encounters almost insuperable difficulties? The answer is clear: Europe had knowledgeable entrepreneurs, skilled workers, an educated citizenry, a body of technical know-how. Well-equipped with rich human capital resources, it was no difficult matter to fill the deficiency in the stock of material capital. Even in the United States, it is estimated that $100 put into education will induce a higher growth in productivity than $100 put into plant and equipment.

In addition to the Harrod-Domar growth equation, reference may perhaps usefully be made to a growth equation based on expectations of a rising income. The basis for such expectations lies of course in the continuous growth over time of autonomous investment (Hicks). Rising expectations rest upon an ever-improving technology, a growing and a better-educated labor force. Given such expectations, transcending the shorter waves of optimism and pessimism of the cycle, we can say that today's income is a function of yesterday's income. The expectational trend will determine at what rate today's income will exceed yesterday's income. The equation is as follows: $\frac{Y_1}{Y_0} = \frac{c+s}{c}$. Y_1 is today's income, Y_0 yesterday's income. Starting from the Harrod-Domar equation, $g = \frac{s}{c}$, we assume that $s = 0.12$, $c = 3$, and so the rate of growth is 0.04.

[3] See Theodore W. Schultz *et al.*, "Investment in Human Beings," *The Journal of Political Economy*, October, 1962.

Applying the same figures to our expectational equation, we get

$$\frac{Y_1}{Y_0} = \frac{c + s}{c} = \frac{3 + 0.12}{3} = 1.04.^4$$

The rate of growth is therefore 4 per cent. The larger the s, the greater is the rate of growth.

Summary Statement on the Role of c and s

At the risk of repetition, a summary view of the growth problem may perhaps be in order. First of all, let us keep in mind that, in dealing with c and s, we are involved in the multiplier-accelerator analysis. This is true because the strength of the accelerator depends upon the capital-output ratio, and the multiplier is the reciprocal of the marginal propensity to save, i.e., $k = \frac{1}{s}$. But although any equation which uses c and s necessarily encounters the problem of demand creation (i.e., the multiplier-accelerator interaction), its primary usefulness relates not to the level of income but to the growth of income.

From the standpoint of generating adequate aggregate demand, the larger the c and the smaller the s, the more expansionist will be the spontaneous forces—forces which are exogenous to the system but whose impact upon the system will be determined (given the strength of the initial jolt) by the endogenous or internal structure of the system itself (namely the multiplier-accelerator interaction). A small s means a powerful multiplier, and a large c a buoyant accelerator. A small s and a large c will *tend* to give us a full-employment economy.

But from the standpoint of growth, the matter is entirely different—the larger the s and the smaller the c, the higher the potential rate of growth. But this growth cannot be achieved without a strong deliberate policy of full employment. If we must rely primarily upon spontaneous forces, we will be better off with a small s and a large c and be content with a low rate of growth. If we can count on strong deliberate policy, we would be better

---

[4] See R. C. O. Matthews, *The Business Cycle*, Cambridge Economic Handbooks, The University of Chicago Press, 1959. Matthews makes his expectational growth equation $\frac{c}{c - s}$. This is approximately right but not quite. Using the figures just given, from his equation, we get the answer 1.0417, not 1.04.

off with a large s and a small c which, under contrived full employment, would promise a high rate of growth.

Is there perhaps something here which has a bearing on the low rate of growth in the United States and the high rate of growth in Europe?

A high s means a large flow of saving if full-employment levels can be reached. And if c is small, this large flow of saving can finance a highly productive (high-output) stock of capital. The smaller the capital-output ratio, the more potent is a given amount of saving; in other words, the further a given amount of capital will go. A large c and a small s are ideal for demand creation but unfavorable from the standpoint of growth.

The Circular-flow Economy vs. a Growing Economy

In a circular-flow economy (Schumpeter) there is no net investment and so no growth. There is indeed a stock of capital, but no additions to this stock are being made. As old capital wears out, it is replaced by new capital. Thus the whole income is spent on consumers' goods. The income received by the factors of production today in return for their productive effort is spent tomorrow on tomorrow's output. And since there is no growth, tomorrow's output is equal to today's output, which in turn is equal to today's income. Income equals expenditures, and expenditures equal income. $Y_0 = E_1 = Y_1$.

In a growing society, however, net investment must be made. If this net investment is stable (no increase), the output will rise, but at a declining rate. If the investment is stable, however, then income will remain fixed. Out of each year's income a certain amount is saved, an amount equal to investment. Thus all the income received today is expended tomorrow, partly on investment and the rest on consumers' goods. The savings of today are expended on investment tomorrow. $I = S$. Income remains constant. But since output is rising (owing to the continuous process of new investment), demand is insufficient to buy the growing output. Thus such a society suffers the depressing effect of deflation or falling prices. Demand and supply are not in equilibrium.

To have growth there must be net investment. And to maintain equilibrium in a growing society, a constant rate of investment will not do. Investment must grow; investment made tomorrow must exceed the saving out of today's income. I_1 must exceed S_0. The difference must be financed out of the activation of idle hoards or out of the creation of new money. Growth must be financed from credit or net increases in debt.

In all modern dynamic societies, debt (public and private) is an increasing function of growth. Aggregate debt (public and private combined) has remained from 1929 to the present at approximately a constant ratio of GNP. The relevant data decade by decade are as follows:

Aggregate Debt and GNP
(*in billions*)

Year	Aggregate Net Debt —Public and Private	Debt as a Multiple of GNP	Individual Debt	Corporate Debt	State and Local Debt	Federal Government Debt	GNP
1929	$ 191	1.83	$ 72	$ 89	13	16	$104
1940	190	1.89	53	76	16	45	101
1950	490	1.72	109	142	21	219	285
1963	1,000	1.81	341	331	72	257	554

5 · *Inflation and the Balance of Payments*

In recent years, the United States has been bedeviled by two problems that limit our freedom of action: the fear of inflation and our international balance of payments. Undoubtedly, they are serious problems which must be dealt with effectively. Unfortunately, however, it is also true that irresponsible groups have exploited these problems for propaganda. Expansionist and social welfare programs have had to encounter not only the opposition of rigid conservatism against progressive measures as such, but also the argument that, even though justified on their own merits, these programs cannot be implemented under existing circumstances without endangering domestic price stability and, internationally, the soundness of the dollar.

The remedies proffered to prevent inflation and to safeguard the dollar have too often assumed that the only effective cure is the continued maintenance of semistagnation. Admittedly, a depressed economy need have no fear of inflation, but is this defeatist policy the only solution? And can continual semistagnation really make the American economy competitive in world markets?

What does history tell us about American experience with inflation? One must say first that, throughout our entire history, this country has never suffered any price increases that remotely deserve the name of inflation except in wartime or in the immediate aftermath of war. And this also holds for our recent postwar experience.

Immediately following the war—1946 and much of 1947—we did indeed have sharp increases in the general price level. Wholesale prices rose by 50 per cent from 1945 to 1948. This price rise was a consequence of the war. At the end of the war, cupboards and closets were empty, retailers' shelves were bare, business firms were short on inventory stocks; there was a terrific shortage of houses (young couples had to double up with their parents), automobile production had been cut almost to zero. During the war, monetary savings had accumulated in the hands of both consumers and business firms. Once price control was removed, prices inevitably rose. The surprising thing was not that prices rose. The surprising thing was rather that, after nine months, the main inflationary upsurge rapidly subsided. Many an economist who had looked for dire inflation was astonished to discover how quickly it had dwindled away. By the end of 1947, it was all over. But people needed some considerable time to find that out, so firmly had the notion become ingrained that inflation was the new order of the day. In fact, however, the last month of 1948 gave us a price level slightly below that of January, 1948. And two years later, the average index of wholesale prices for the year 1950 stood 1 per cent lower than the average for the year 1948.

In midsummer 1950, the Korean war broke out. The whole world was shocked. All over western Europe and in the United States prices rose in nine months by about 15 per cent. Consumers rushed out to buy electrical appliances, cars, etc. Business firms hastily stocked up with inventories. Once again, the surprising thing was how rapidly the inflationary fever vanished. By February, 1951, it was all over, and prices began to recede. The wholesale price index for 1952 stood 3 per cent below that of 1951, and there was a further decline of $1\frac{1}{2}$ per cent by 1953.

And what has been our peacetime record since Korea? Except for the investment boom of 1955–57, wholesale prices have held stable. Wholesale prices did indeed rise an average of 2.2 per cent per year from 1954 to 1957. Historically, we have typically experienced moderate price increases of this order of magnitude in the expansionist phase of the business cycle. Indeed in the nine cycles from 1894 to 1913, and from 1921 to 1929, the average increase in wholesale prices per year of expansion was 3.5 per cent. Moreover the 1955–57 episode was a special case. The price increases were restricted mainly to the capital goods sector—metals, machinery, construction. In the economy as a whole there was no inflation.

This investment boom did, however, leave its imprint on the wholesale price level. From 1957 to 1963, the index remained stable but on this new high plateau. Even so, in 1963, the wholesale price index stood only 6 per cent above the 1952 index—an increase for the eleven years of only one-half of 1 per cent per year. Everyone must agree that this represents not only "reasonable" price stability, but stability of a very high order. Compare this record with the price increase of 2.5 per cent per year from 1897 to 1915 —the good old peacetime days! Of course there was the Spanish-American War, but its role was minor and short-lived compared with the sweep of economic factors which brought about the worldwide upward price trend.

But this is the record of wholesale prices. How about consumer prices? Here we come closer to a real problem. The consumer price index has not done so well. Yet the record is far better than the inflation-alarmists would have us believe. Consumer prices were pushed up along with wholesale prices by the shock of Korea. And from 1952 to 1963, the increase has aggregated 15 per cent.

Why this greater rise in consumer prices? The explanation can mainly be found in the "service" sector. From 1957 to 1963, the price of services rose by 14 per cent while the commodity sector rose by only 5 per cent. And in the service area by far the greatest increases have come in medical care—a 20 per cent increase since 1957.

In general, the price index for services can be expected to rise even though the commodity sector is stabilized. This will occur because productivity increases in the commodity sector permit price stability even though money wages rise in line with productivity increases. That is not true in the case of services. Here productivity gains are meager, yet wages must rise more or less in line with general nationwide increases. Accordingly, the price index for services is pushed up out of line with the commodity price index.

Not much can be done about this, even though the special case of medical and hospital services deserves attention. This problem, however, lies beyond the scope of this chapter. For our purposes here, the important question to ask is this: Given the unquestioned fact that the consumer price index tends to outstrip the wholesale price index, which index should we try to stabilize?

Assume that we successfully stabilized the consumer price index. This implies a downward trend in wholesale prices. Is this desirable from the standpoint of the economy? The answer is "No." The wholesale price index is a matter of deep concern for business and for farmers. Continuous wholesale price deflation would put a squeeze, probably an intolerable squeeze, upon the entrepreneurial class.[1] The conclusion is that we should plump for stability of wholesale prices. But this means that we must expect a continuous upward trend in the consumer price index. An increase in the consumer price index of 1 to 2 per cent per year, such as we have had since 1957, is tolerable and perhaps more or less inevitable. Even the more rigid stabilizers have come to regard increases of this magnitude as "reasonable stability."

The record has therefore on the whole been good since the end of the Korean conflict, except for the years 1955–57. But here we encounter an alarming fact. These were just the years when the unemployment rate fell close to the Kennedy goal of 4 per cent. In all other post-Korean years, the unemployment rate has averaged from 5.6 to 6.8 per cent, and in no year did it fall below 5.5 per cent. Does this mean that we can buy price stability only at the cost of 5.6 per cent unemployment?

No conclusive answer can be given, but the following comments may be pertinent. The 1955–57 episode represented a sharp spurt in the durable-goods sector. Admittedly, this is typically the

---

[1] Of course, if we could assume perfect mobility of factors, perfect competition, and perfect fluidity of all prices and costs, a continuous fall in prices would make no great difference. But this is not the kind of world we live in; indeed, it is a world that never existed except in the minds of highly speculative economists.

case in the boom phase of the cycle. Yet this appears to have been an extreme case. The exceptional spurt in auto sales and other consumers' durables, the spurt in the capital goods industries was the result of pent-up demand accumulations occasioned by the war and by rapid postwar technological developments. Normally, we could expect a more balanced recovery. Moreover, we could do a better job of stabilizing private spending both for investment goods and consumers' durables than we have thus far attempted. This matter has already been discussed in Chapters 1 and 2. Discretionary adjustment of tax rates to stabilize the cycle could go a long way toward shifting the so-called modified Phillips curve [2] downward. Similarly the removal or lessening of structural bottlenecks via educational and retraining programs could also help to shift the Phillips curve downward or to the left.

Finally, price stability involves statesman-like collective bargaining. On the average, money wage rates can rise no faster than productivity increases permit. These matters were explored with some care in the writer's *Economic Policy and Full Employment*, published in 1946.[3] Broadly speaking we can very roughly divide industries into three classes: (1) those making average increases in per worker productivity, (2) those making exceptionally large increases in productivity, and (3) those making very small increases in productivity. The first group can raise wages equal to productivity increases while holding prices stable. The second can raise wages equal to, or perhaps somewhat above, the general average productivity increases, while lowering prices to consumers. The third group is compelled to raise wages more or less in line with the national average, and is therefore compelled also to raise prices sufficiently to cover wage costs. In a dynamic society, some prices will fall and some will rise, while others remain stable. If money

---

[2] On the vertical scale put a schedule of price increases ranging from 0 to 8. On the horizontal scale put a schedule of unemployment rates ranging from 0 to 6. Draw a line through the point 8 in the price scale and point 5.5 on the unemployment scale. This line will show a price increase of 1.5 per cent at 4.5 per cent unemployment, and a price rise of 2.2 per cent at a 4 per cent unemployment rate. The Phillips curve purports to show that price increases are a function of the rate of unemployment.

[3] The guidelines for wage increases were extensively discussed in the Report of the Council of Economic Advisers in the *President's Economic Report*, January, 1962.

wages and money increases generally rise in line with productivity, the general price level can remain stable. "Productivity-wages" constitute the backbone of the price level.

Historically, the aggregate share of labor and capital in the final product has remained about equal. Assuming a constant capital-output ratio, a 10 per cent increase in output per worker will mean also a 10 per cent increase per worker in the capital stock. Assume that the yield on capital remains the same. It follows that a 10 per cent increase in output will permit a 10 per cent increase in the income of capitalists. Assume that wages rise percentage-wise as much as output, namely 10 per cent. It follows then that labor's income will have increased 10 per cent per worker. In other words Kr ("K" being the capital invested and "r" the yield per dollar invested) would rise by 10 per cent. Similarly Lw ("L" being the number of workers, and "w" the money wage rate) would also rise by 10 per cent. Thus capital's share would remain constant and labor's share would also remain constant. Broadly speaking, this is what history shows to have been the fact.

In the event that the capital-output ratio should decline, this might result in some drop in capital's share in the growing output. This in fact appears to have been the case to a small degree in the last two or three decades.

Why should the yield on capital (the "r") tend to remain stable while wages (the "w" in our equation) rise along with productivity? The answer is that so long as the stock of capital, K, tends to rise as fast as output per worker, K is obviously becoming plentiful in relation to labor. Under the law of factoral substitution, this means that a unit of capital is becoming cheap while a unit of labor is becoming dear. Thus wages per worker rise in line with productivity whereas the yield on a unit of capital remains constant. But since the stock of capital, K, rises in line with output, capital's share of the growing product continues to hold its own against labor's share.

The Balance-of-Payments Problem

The second roadblock to freedom to pursue full-employment policies is the international position of the dollar. Briefly the story is as follows: For four years following the war (1946–49), we averaged an over-all surplus in our international accounts of $1.75 billion per year. Government grants and credits to foreign countries, averaging around $5.5 billion per year, were more than offset by a gigantic excess of exports over imports [4] of goods and services—an excess of $8.5 billion per year. This huge excess was, of course, to be expected in the immediate postwar period when Europe was still economically speaking flat on its back. But by 1950 things began to change.

For the seven years 1950–56 inclusive, the net excess of exports fell to $4.4 billion per year. Europe was again exporting in volume. Offsetting this surplus were three items: (a) military expenditures abroad ($2.2 billion); (b) United States grants and credits ($2.5 billion); (c) private capital outflows ($1.4 billion). This left an average over-all deficit in our international accounts for these seven years of $1.4 billion per year.

Our gold losses, however, averaged only $0.36 billion per year; hence the adverse balance was accepted without causing any great concern. And in 1957, owing to special factors, particularly the favorable impact of the Suez crisis upon our trade balance, our over-all international account was in surplus by over $0.5 billion.

Thus everything moved satisfactorily until 1958. Then came the crash. Our trade balance ($5.6 billion), although well below the 1957 exceptional year, was $1.2 billion above the previous five years. Nothing wrong there. United States grants and credits abroad held at the seven-year average of $2.5 billion. Military expenditures abroad ($3.4 billion) did exceed the seven-year average by about $1.2 billion. But this was exactly covered by the larger trade surplus. There remain the private capital outflows of $3.0 billion, or $1.6 billion in excess of the 1950–56 average.

The largest increase came in the private capital outflows. Long-term investment, both direct and portfolio, took a big leap forward in 1958. Europe was rapidly expanding. American firms, in line with the buoyant European prosperity, were enlarging their investment outlays on plant and equipment. Europeans needing capital floated a large volume of securities in New York, by far the most favorable capital market in the world. The prospect of early

---

[4] For our present purposes, we place military expenditures abroad in a special category and therefore exclude this item from the import column.

convertibility of European currencies (achieved by late 1958) was also a factor favoring American investment abroad. All in all, our over-all deficit in 1958 was $3.5 billion.

The 1959 deficit of $3.7 billion only slightly exceeded the 1958 deficit. But the composition of the deficit had changed. Private capital outflows declined by $1.0 billion; government grants and credits by $0.5 billion. These were offset by a corresponding reduction in our trade surplus.

The 1960 deficit rose to $3.9 billion. A spectacular recovery in our trade surplus was offset by renewed capital outflows, this time consisting heavily of speculative short-term funds—the so-called hot money.

A determined effort was made to reduce the deficit in 1961, and with a moderate degree of success. The deficit fell to $2.5 billion. A variety of measures was employed—none of outstanding significance but all contributing something. These involved:

1. The assurance that we would use *all* our gold resources if necessary to meet foreign demands.

2. Higher short-term money rates to remove unfavorable interest rate differentials between the United States and Europe.

3. Cutting the tourist allowance for tariff-free purchases from $500 to $100.

4. Tieing our loans to underdeveloped countries to American exports.

5. Efforts to induce Europe to assume more of the foreign-aid burden.

6. Inducing European governments to purchase military equipment in the United States.

7. Federal promotion programs to aid American exports.

These policies, together with advance repayments of loans, brought the 1961 deficit down to $2.5 billion and the 1962 deficit to $1.9 billion. Confidence in the dollar was restored; gold outflows dropped from $2.3 billion in 1958 to $0.9 billion in 1962. In no year has there been an over-all "run" on the dollar. In each year, gold withdrawals have been more than offset by increases in foreign holdings of United States short-term dollar assets—deposits in banks, United States government securities, etc. One cannot talk about a "run on a bank" if fresh deposits considerably exceed currency withdrawals.

Our balance-of-payments deficit is not due to an "unfavorable" trade balance. Our combined net receipts on merchandise and service account have been running at $7.6 billion per year [5] in 1960–62—up about $3 billion above the level of the early fifties. Our problem is rather that the international political situation requires military expenditures abroad amounting to about $3 billion per year, together with net foreign aid of about $3 billion. Add to this an outflow of private long-term and short-term capital of around $3.5 billion. These three items (military expenditures abroad, foreign aid, and capital outflows) tell us that we are supplying foreigners with around $9.5 billion dollars a year outside of the normal channels of trade. Our favorable trade surplus of goods and services of $7.6 billion is not enough to offset the $9.5 billion outflow of dollars. Hence the deficit. It does not mean that United States products are being priced out of world markets.

The balance-of-payments problem is not only a headache for the United States. It almost perennially concerns Great Britain. It is chronically a concern for the underdeveloped countries, and potentially a cause of concern for all countries. The free world should somehow learn to manage its international monetary relations far better than it has so far succeeded in doing. What if anything can be done about it?

Two quite distinct problems confront us: One relates to liquidity; that problem is how to provide an *amount* of international monetary reserves adequate to meet the requirements of international payments. The other problem has to do with maintaining a balanced structure of foreign exchange rates and keeping it continually in balance.

With respect to the first problem, international monetary reserves consist of gold holdings and liquid asset holdings (deposits and short-term securities) of key currencies—mainly the United States dollar and the British pound. Other currencies—the Ger-

---

[5] Remember that United States military expenditures abroad are not included in the "import" category. Logically, that item deserves a separate classification along with foreign aid, etc.

man mark, the Swiss franc, etc.—are beginning to play the same role. Holding liquid assets of gold and key currencies (generally accepted all over the world) enables a country to pay its foreign bills. The problem of adequate international liquidity involves an adequate gold supply plus an adequate volume of key currency holdings. Gold and key currency holdings can, however, be supplemented by borrowings, especially borrowings from the International Monetary Fund.

The aggregate volume of International Monetary reserves is equal to about $60 billion. World trade increases at about a 5 per cent rate per year. This means that around $3 billion new "international money" is needed each year in a growing, dynamic world. Where will this come from? About $1 billion can come from new gold production. The rest must come from (a) an increase in the holdings of key currencies, (b) increased potential borrowings from the International Monetary Fund, or (c) an increase in the price of gold. Any other source must await drastic monetary innovations.

The growing volume of dollar holdings by foreigners has contributed greatly to international liquidity. In 1950, we held a disproportionate share of the world's gold. We still held in 1963 about $16 billion out of a total of $41 billion of free world gold stocks. As a result of new gold production and the United States deficits, foreign countries have steadily increased their holdings of gold and dollars until by 1963 their aggregate holdings of monetary reserves amounted to $42 billion.

Some economists hold that gold production, key currencies, and an expanding role of the International Monetary Fund as an international lender will not be sufficient to provide adequate liquidity. Two widely advocated solutions are offered. Sir Roy Harrod favors a drastic increase in the price of gold. If this were done worldwide, say, through the auspices of the International Monetary Fund as permitted in its charter, it would in no way disturb the structure of exchange rates. The only effect would be an increase in the monetary value of gold. A doubling of the price of gold would simply mean that current world gold stocks, instead of being worth $41 billion in money terms would be worth $82 billion.

A second method of increasing international liquidity would require a shift from the current key currency type of international monetary reserves to a strictly international kind of money. Keynes called his proposed new international money the "bancor." Whatever the name, this new international monetary unit would supplant the key currencies. It would be issued by a truly international central bank. This bank would not simply be a lending agency like a savings bank—lending out funds deposited with it —as is now true of the International Monetary Fund. The new truly international bank would have the power to *create* new international money precisely as our own Federal Reserve System can do with respect to domestic currency. The Federal Reserve can and does create new dollars. It does so by buying United States securities in the open market and paying for them by checks drawn on itself which, if so desired, can be cashed into new Federal Reserve notes. The money supply has thus been increased. If the bonds were purchased from a comercial bank, this bank would be credited for the amount of the purchase with a deposit at the Federal Reserve Bank. In this way, member bank balances with the Federal Reserve Banks would rise, and thereby make possible a multiple expansion of the money supply. In precisely the same manner, an international central bank could create "bancor" by buying the government securities of any member country.

A mere increase in liquidity will not, however, solve the balance-of-payments problem. For this relates, at least in the long run, not to a country's supply of international monetary reserves, but to disequilibrium forces which are continuously at work causing a drain on its reserves. Larger reserves can, of course, tide a country over a period of *temporary* disequilibrium, but cannot cure a *fundamental* disequilibrium.

International equilibrium can be maintained in two ways. One involves unilateral action by each country to keep its cost and price level in line with those of other countries, to broaden if possible the range of its exports, to develop its own industries so as to minimize its need for imports, etc. Moreover, international collaboration on simultaneous expansionist policies can help to keep each country in step. Self-discipline and international co-operation are both involved.

The other method of maintaining equilibrium involves continuous adjustment of the exchange rate structure so as to maintain the value of each country's currency in terms of world markets and internationally traded financial assets. The exchange rate of the dollar, for example, would fluctuate according to changes in the world demand for dollars. In other words, the exchange rate would vary so as to maintain the purchasing power of the dollar in the world commodity and securities market.

This ideal cannot be reached all at once, but we are moving in this direction. The problem is building up the institutional machinery needed for a managed international monetary system. In fact, in many of the advanced countries there is being built up what, in effect, amounts to national stabilization funds equipped with the power to buy and sell their own currencies against other currencies. This means controlling, through sales and purchases, the exchange value of currencies within the limits of the selling and buying gold points. The current range within which exchange rates fluctuate is 1½ percentage points. This could bit by bit be widened to say five or more percentage points, within which a managed exchange rate could be allowed to fluctuate. In time, international cooperation between the national stabilization funds could dispense altogether with gold, just as all modern domestic currencies are no longer dependent upon gold.

Our money supply, and so the value of money, is no longer determined by a gold standard. Our money supply is completely controlled by the Governors of the Federal Reserve Board without any regard to gold. At long last, we have achieved management of our domestic monetary system. We must achieve international monetary management. Increasing cooperation between the central banks of advanced countries and a growing role for the International Monetary Fund point the way toward eventual international management comparable to domestic monetary management.

Many of the current schemes of international monetary reform are simply plans to support the glutted currencies of the deficit countries, notably the United States and Great Britain. At best, such schemes serve only to tide a country over a temporary difficulty without doing much if anything to promote equilibrium.

What is needed is an orderly management of exchange rates so that the various currencies will represent *true* values in goods, services, and assets. Not until this is done will a country be wholly free to tackle effectively the problem of keeping its economy continuously close to full employment without periodic lapses from its full growth potential.

Index